To Ren

HAPPY BIRTHDAY

from

Dad

Feb 97

THE CONTROVERSIAL COLENSOS

THE
CONTROVERSIAL
COLENSOS

A.L. ROWSE

First published 1989
© A.L. Rowse 1989

ISBN 1–85022–047–6

Published by *Dyllansow Truran*
Cornish Publications
Trewolsta, Trewirgie, Redruth, Cornwall

Production Consultant Anthony Wheaton, Tedburn St. Mary, Devon, UK.
0647 61 329

Printed by Bookcraft Ltd., Midsomer Norton, Somerset, UK.

Preface

My motive in writing this duo-biography is to do justice to two remarkable Cornishmen who are overlooked today. People are apt to pass over Cornish folk: for years I have done my best to make other people aware of our existence. In the United States few know of the distinctive contribution the Cornish have made to building up the greatest of the English-speaking peoples – though I have done my bit with *The Cornish in America*.

Bishop Colenso of Natal was a celebrated figure in the 19th century, indeed notorious as the greatest Biblical scholar in Britain in his time. He is still little appreciated as such today. But in South Africa he is remembered as the gallant defender of the blacks, and rightly revered by the Zulus for his heart-breaking struggle on their behalf.

His cousin William Colenso was the first of New Zealand naturalists, to whom this country owed thousands of seeds, and hundreds of plants. He was the prime authority on New Zealand flora, and intrepid explorer of the North Island. Starting as missionary and printer, he translated and printed many books for the Maoris, of whom he in his turn was an interpreter and defender.

I wonder whether these men's sympathy with, and struggles for, the underdog may not have been due, unconsciously, to their inheritance from their own small, submerged people – though still alive and kicking.

A.L. Rowse.

St. Austell, Cornwall.

Dedication

To
Robert Eliot of St Germans
in friendship
and for his work for Cornwall

Book I

John William Colenso of Natal

Chapter I
Two Cousins

John William Colenso (1814–1883), Bishop of Natal, and William Colenso of New Zealand (1811–1899), each made a distinctive and striking contribution to the age in which he lived. The Bishop won world-wide fame—at the time notoriety, rather—as a foremost figure in Biblical criticism in the century, in England its leading exponent. He won a second fame—and again much unpopularity and vilification—as the friend and defender of the blacks in South Africa, particularly of Langalibalele and King Cetewayo of Zululand in their troubles. William Colenso was even more intimate with the Maoris, whose language he mastered—and spent years compiling a dictionary of it—as his cousin mastered Zulu and published both a grammar and a dictionary, besides many translations. Even more, William Colenso became the first of New Zealand naturalists, sending hundreds, if not thousands, of new plants and seeds to Kew and home to Cornwall.

They both were intensely controversial figures. The Bishop on a world-wide scale, along with Darwin and Huxley, for his revelation of the true nature of the Old Testament, as the literature of the ancient Jews, with its folk-tales and myths, its contradictions and impossibilities, exaggerations and mistakes as to numbers, dates, sequence of events—like any other ancient literature, Greek or Roman. This made him anathema to thousands, condemned by a public quite unqualified to pronounce on the question, unaware that it was unable to think, strictly speaking, let alone judge. For the scholar's findings were essentially unanswerable—and went unanswered for all the hullaballoo—and are now accepted by all intelligent people as common sense on the subject. By the blacks of South Africa his name is remembered with esteem—Sobantu, Father of the People; the centenary of his death properly commemorated a few years ago in Natal, if not in oblivious Britain.

3

William Colenso's controversies were personal and local—
perhaps we should say, provincial. They broke his career in
two; for, a missionary in deacon's orders, he involved himself
with a seductive Maori girl in the house. He was determined to
hold on to the boy, fruit of the liaison, when the mother
wanted to take him back to her clan; there was a contest for his
possession—thus the scandal became public. William was
drummed out of the mission field and lay low for a few years;
then built himself a successful new career in trading and
politics, local and provincial (or national, according to taste).
He became a member of the legislative assembly, inspector of
schools, governmental treasurer, what not. He ended, if not in
the odour of sanctity, at least in the fragrance of prosperity.

Both Colensos were up to their eyes in controversial issues;
and could not have avoided some controversy, if they had
wished. They did not wish. Some element in their personalities
must have sought a challenge, as well as provoked it. They
were doughty fighters, convinced that they were right—as they
largely were—and would never give up or give in, when they
had their world against them. Though they hardly knew each
other—their life's work kept them half the world apart and
they cannot have met after their earliest years—they have
certain characteristics in common. Over many years I have
thought of deciphering them, descrying the common elements
in their very individual personalities. They themselves would
be unaware of this, in the Victorian way, in spite of the
distance between them, socially as well as geographically; and
also, in spite of various contrasting circumstances.

To take the most significant contrast at once. The Bishop's
marriage was a love-match, his wife a remarkable woman, his
intellectual equal, who made herself his helpmeet all her life.
They had an ideally happy family life, their children—
especially the girls, Harriet and Frances—much above average
intelligence: all of them identified with their father's causes,
and helping notably to advance them. And all of them writing
like mad.

William Colenso's family life was miserable. Neither husband nor wife loved or much liked, the other. After the birth of
two children they gave up sex relations, and William consoled
himself for a time with his willing Repeka. Then she rebelled

and wanted to take their son away with her to her people. William loved his half-caste boy, Willie, who grew up to be a handsome sailor and ultimately settled in his father's native Penzance. The eminent naturalist does not seem to have got much fun out of sex or family life. His wife took their children, away with her, and William settled into a somewhat solitary, querulous life, projecting his dissatisfaction, and his undoubted abilities, into public controversy.

The overriding external circumstance that Bishop and Deacon had in common was that they were missionary enthusiasts, deeply devoted to the mission field—incredibly to us, in our age and generation. It is hard for us to understand the strength of the impulse that in the 19th century drove such people to lives of hardship and danger, in remote countries among primitive peoples, some of them savages, like those who killed the first bishop of Melanesia. Perhaps it is even more incomprehensible when it comes to ancient civilisations like those of India and China, which had attained upper reaches of culture when Northern Europe was still barbarian. When one contrasts the ineffable non-dogmatism of Buddism or the rational commonsense of Confucianism with the nonsense-propositions of Christian metaphysics, to preach the latter to the former would seem impertinent, and certainly without a sense of humour.

The unsectarian historian can see the astonishing energy put forth in Christian missionary activity as part and parcel of European secular expansion, in trade and commerce, ecomomic and political imperialism, with their concomitant conflicts.

Naturally missonaries—unselfaware, as most people are—did not see things like this. They were believers: they had a Gospel to preach. (It is men's beliefs that make fools of them or, rather, that corroborate and strengthen the innate foolery in them.) The Bishop's intelligent wife said that, ever since she had first met her husband, she had known him possessed with the idea of becoming a missionary to the heathen. She herself did not fancy leaving her familiar Norfolk for the unknown quantity of Natal. What she did know was that her sister, married to a missionary, lost five children in six years in the appalling climate of Borneo.

Nevertheless, such was the strength of her husband's urge, the devotion of his personality, the love between them, that she consented to go out, with their four children, and take on all the risks and dangers with him. She came to love Natal, as he did, and regarded the place they created, Bishopstowe, with its garden and view of mountain and sea, as 'a little paradise'. She spent forty years there, the Bishop thirty. When he died, she would not come back home to England: 'home' was Natal. There she remained with her daughters, the family unit still fighting his causes, for which, worn out, he fell before his 70th year.

The Deacon was already in the mission-field in New Zealand, some twenty years ahead of his cousin. There he remained for the rest of his life, over sixty years, dying at the patriarchal age of 88, on the very threshold of this century.

How much they had in common! They were fanatically Protestant, hating the encroachment of Victorian ritualism, each of them fighting a rearguard action against the advance of the Oxford Movement in re-Catholicising the old-fashioned Church of England. The Deacon had his conflict with his High Church Bishop Selwyn, first bishop of New Zealand, as his cousin had his with Bishop Gray, first bishop of Cape Town.

Here the episcopal John William had an advantage over plain William. In those days it was something to be a lord bishop, Lord Bishop of Natal, and the junior in years moved in the best society as such, not only in South Africa but whenever he returned to England, in spite of his notoriety and the outcry of the orthodox against him. He had his supporters, few as they were among the higher clergy; but Dean Stanley and Jowett of Balliol were with him, so were Tennyson and Carlyle, the eminent geologist Lyell, Huxley and most of the scientists. These were the people he moved among on his visits home.

Nothing of that in William's life, though he was for many years a correspondent of the great naturalists, the Hookers, and met the young Darwin, when the *Beagle* made a landfall in New Zealand.

In fact one notices a certain class difference. William was not a university man: he began life as a poor printer, a tradesman. John William, D.D., was a university man, Fellow of St John's College, Cambridge, and all that. He was very much a gentleman, married into a social stratum—the Bignolds, Bickersteths and Bunyons of Norfolk—much above the Colensos of Penzance, who were lower middle-class, neither upper, nor working-class.

They had a respectable provenance. There had been Colensos in Penzance from the time the parish registers of Madron began, the Elizabethan age. I rather fancy that the foreign sound of the name Colenso aided the notoriety it came to have—enough to frighten old ladies who thought that the Bible was written by the Hand of God, if incapable of understanding that the Pentateuch was not written by the hand of Moses.

Actually Colenso is an intelligible Cornish name, coming from the neighbouring parish of St Hilary, where there are a couple of farms (not 'estates', as over-impressed colonials describe them): Higher and Lower Colenso. Co or Ke = wall; lyn = pool; so or dhu = dark; hence the name referred to a dark pool by a wall or hedge, as we say, on the place.

It is a more chancy matter to descry Cornish characteristics in the cousins. If I were to make the attempt, I should denote the mania for work each of them had—work, work, work: scribble, scribble, scribble; preach, preach, preach. There was Methodism in the Colenso family. One of the uncles was a life-long local preacher. Both cousins had a fling with Methodism when young, though ultimately opting for the dear old Church of England. But their conception of it was an exclusively, aggressively Protestant one; each of them thought he was fighting the battle of the Reformation again, against priestcraft and for the liberation of the spirit from the trammels, and absurdities, of orthodoxy. Luther was a hero to both. (I do not share their prejudices). William even went so far as to call his (legitimate) son, Ridley Latimer. Neither Colenso had a sense of humour—and the Cornish sense of humour is certainly peculiar.

Nor had they much sense of tact—too downright, and undeviatingly, indestructibly *honest*—I should diagnose, to a fault. The Bishop was a great gentleman, and in time became an indubitably great man. I doubt if we can call the Deacon altogether a gentleman, though he had some gentlemanly qualities. He was too outspoken, and too personal—true, he had had a lot to contend with. The Bishop had too—and yet never spoke out against his enemies, or would allow any reference to what he inwardly felt. His wife knew, and put it all down to meekness—a Victorian value I do not much care for. I wonder whether it was not rather an inner pride that withheld the Bishop, as well as a Christian spirit that made him refrain from describing his opponents as the fools they were. Someone should have told them the score—that the third-rate do not qualify to hold an opinion on such matters as Biblical scholarship, any more than on the Sonnets of Shakespeare or the crimes of Richard III. They do not know what they are talking about.

However, Bishop Colenso did have entire intellectual confidence in himself, and rightly. When he began his scholarly investigation of the Old Testament, there was no scholarship worthy of the name on the subject in England. It was all in German, and Colenso had to learn German—he already knew Hebrew; and, though he was a brilliant mathematician, he actually preferred classics. He was the initiator of modern Biblical Criticism in England, working away like a mole entirely on his own, in Natal. A modern authority tells us that Colenso's *Pentateuch* is 'one of the most original British contributions to Biblical criticism in the whole 19th century, and has a signal importance for the history of the subject as a whole.'[1]

Colenso must have known that perfectly well; nobody could produce an answer to his findings (any more than to mine on Shakespeare). All that they could do was to abuse the scholar, round and about the subject, *without ever going into it*—though that they were incapable of doing. The good Bishop never pointed that out to them—and it is always a duty to do so, however unpopular that may be, for how otherwise are the third-rate to learn?

He had fortitude to support him in his uphill fight; but he evidently had an inner intellectual pride to support him. For he knew that he, the first-rate scholar on the subject was right, and the third-rate, the eminent hypocrites and humbugs, as well as ordinary humans, were wrong as usual. Even the great Renan, who had similar troubles to put up with from the

1.　John Rogerson, *Old Testament Criticism in the Nineteenth Century*, 220 foll.

orthodox all his life, particularly over his *Vie de Jésus*, wrote patronisingly that Colenso had written before he resolved his doubts. It was Mrs Colenso who took up her pen and wrote to the great man—a fellow-Celt, by the way—that her husband hadn't written from any *doubts*: he was quite certain in his views.

Evidently both cousins were markedly individualistic, as they were striking individuals. William spoke out, and answered fools according to their folly; the Bishop, never. I cannot but think that this was a mistake; for when ultimately—not until after his death—his work was absorbed and accepted as he must have known it would be, his achievement was then overlooked and himself forgotten.

A rugged individualism is true of Cornish people— understandably from the long isolation of Cornish society through history, the small isolated hamlets, lonely farms and cottages; even in my early days there was no centricity in village life. What sociality there was congregated around the Methodist chapels. And we must certainly impute the over-riding sense of mission to the Colensos' religious belief. The Bishop's whole life was ruled by his belief in the Fatherhood of God and the Brotherhood of Man (today!). To this we must add his extreme conscientiousness, the scrupulousness as evident in his scholarship as in his life. He constantly revised his work, and his views on specific points; one notes the development from his first devastating volume of criticism of the Pentateuch, to the later volumes. Our leading authority today notes the increase in sensitivity over the decade he devoted to the work—prodigious as it was, seven volumes in ten years!

The Deacon also was a conscientious man, untiring in duty; I doubt if he was as sensitively scrupulous as his cousin. Paradoxically, he was more autocratic, and brusque, where the Bishop was paternal and gentle. He was also strangely optimistic; he held the rationalist's view that a question need only be rationally stated and logically argued for people to see the reason of it. An historian knows people better than that: I have always denominated that view as the Rationalist Fallacy.

Naturally, holding this view, the Bishop was surprised by the strength of the reaction, the hatred his book provoked. To the orthodox and conventional he became a Monster—'that dreadful Colenso' to Charlotte M. Yonge, High Church author of many novels to improve young ladies; and to the public in general, a caricature, frequently depicted in *Punch*, and by 'Spy'.

Both Colensos were tactless. Even the Bishop's wife, who upheld him in all his views and ways, occasionally suggested that he might be more 'reticent', and perhaps a bit more tolerant of opposition and incomprehension. He always replied that the duty lay upon him to speak out the truth, and nothing but the truth. I do not think he ever deviated from this; he was quite unyielding—though, if convinced of a mistake, he no less scrupulously conceded it. I am not sure that one could say this for the Deacon.

No evidence remains of any contacts between them—one for sixty years in far New Zealand, the other for thirty in not quite so out-of-touch Natal. William in New Zealand read something of his famous cousin's works, for we find him citing the Bishop's exposure of rigid Sabbatarianism.

We come back to the common foundation of their life's work as missionaries, and an important influence it takes a Cornishman to observe. In the previous generation their fellow Cornishman, Henry Martyn (1781–1812), won fame for the remarkable work he accomplished in India during his brief life. Always delicate, he nevertheless went out and sacrificed life to it. In his few years in Bengal, in addition to his religious and educational work, he translated the New Testament into Hindustani, then into Persian, with a second improved version to follow; he translated the Prayer Book into Hindustani, the Psalms into Persian, the gospels into Judaeo-Persic. Martyn was a brilliant scholar, a Senior Wrangler and 1st Smith's Prizeman, then Fellow of St John's. John William Colenso went up to St John's became Second Wrangler and Smith's Prizeman, then Fellow of the College

It is impossible to doubt that Henry Martyn's life and career had its influence. There was a cult of him in Cornwall, where he has always been remembered. (An All Souls friend of mine saw his tomb in the interior of Asia Minor a few years ago; Martyn died on his way overland back to England: he was only thirty.) A Memoir of him came out in 1819; then his *Journals and Letters* were edited by Bishop Wilberforce—of all people. *He* never ventured abroad into the mission field, but prospered at home as bishop of Oxford then Winchester, and led the episcopal campaign against Colenso.

Meanwhile William went out to New Zealand in 1833. It was not until 1853 that his cousin was free of his difficulties, mainly financial, to enter upon the career that had long held his heart and mind.

Chapter II
Cornwall—Cambridge—Norfolk

Though the Colensos were solid Penzance people, John William was born at my native St Austell on 24 January 1814.[1] His mother, a Cornish Blackmore, his father, also John William, was the brother of the Deacon's father. St Austell parish was rich in minerals, and the Bishop's father ventured his capital in what he described as 'The Happy Union Tin Stream Works at Pentewan' in a geological journal in 1829. This place is a beautiful valley lying southward between St Austell and the sea. But it was far from happy—the sea flooded in, engulfed the works and Colenso *père* lost all his capital.

Little is known of him thereafter, except that he made do as a mineral agent for the Duchy of Cornwall, and died at Plymouth in 1864. There used to be a window pane scratched with the initials J.W.C. in the house at Elm Terrace where they lived. Here the mother died when John was a boy of fifteen, her 'dying eyes resting upon him', leaving the care of his brothers and sisters to *him*. Always serious-minded, never a thought or any time for play, essentially literal in mind, John took the charge literally. In spite of his own harrowing struggle, he later managed to educate a clever younger brother, who became a Fellow of Exeter College, Oxford. Thereupon he died, at Lostwithiel; there is a window commemorating his ability and promise, in his college chapel.

Meanwhile John himself was keen to get to the university. 'May the Lord preserve me from despondency and despair', he wrote as a youth, 'for I candidly confess I am fit for nothing else but the university.' There was no money for it, so at seventeen he took a job as usher in a private school, working from 5.30 a.m. until 8 p.m. On £20 a year he managed to save, then his relatives raised a loan of £30 for a first year at

1. It is not known for certain where in the parish Colenso was born, probably at Pondu in the Pentewan Valley.

Cambridge. He won a sizarship at St John's, which meant the privilege of dining off the orts and ends after the Fellows had gorged themselves at high table. He supplemented this by private teaching and publishing translations of Plato and Horace, rising early and staying up into the night for his own studies. Result: 'I have hardly ate or slept for the last week, and am afraid I am looking "like a winnard", as we say, through anxiety and fatigue.' 'Winnard' is our dialect word for peewit; 'like a dying winnard' we say when the birds come down about the house starving in frosty winters.

I am impressed when I read of the struggle these young fellows went through to get an education in those days—though my own chance was narrow enough earlier this century. Really, I have no patience with the complaints people make today, when everything is done for them: they should try a little self-help, instead of expecting the welfare state and everybody else to support them.

Shortly Colenso won himself prizes and an exhibition, which enabled him to stay the course. He emerged with a brilliant degree, Second Wrangler in the Mathematics Tripos and Second Smith's Prizeman out of the whole university. In 1837 he was elected a Fellow: he was home.

A Fellowship meant security, but did not in itself bring in much money. So he took on a tutorship at Harrow, which, with the running of a house, was well paid, but not congenial. 'I am very solitary in the midst of a crowd. . . I walk, ride, sit and think alone.'

Once more the Colenso ill-luck struck. The big house and all that he had put into it went up in flames, leaving him with the enormous debt of £5000. Nothing for it but to go back to College and the dreary grind of endless teaching mathematics to the unwilling. To this, now ordained, he added preaching—and here at Cambridge his dry, factual style seems to have been appreciated. He began to be in request as a preacher. However, he found a more remunerative outlet, if somewhat deadening, in writing mathematical text-books. These took on, and made money—which went painfully towards meeting his mountain of debt. Still, he had found a more paying vein than his father had done in his 'Happy Union' tin stream. Thousands of people knew his name from

Colenso's Arithmetic, throughout the Victorian age, before it became darkened by its Biblical associations. Longmans made a fortune out of his text-books, if he did not.

It was during these years of sloggging, always anxious and always arduous, that Colenso met Frances Bunyon and life brightened for him. She belonged to a well-to-do-Norwich family, a cheerful family life with relations extending in every direction. John wrote to her pathetically, 'I have never had a Home, where I could taste its real character, or test its capabilities for joy or sorrow.' It seems an odd way of putting it, when they had both fallen in love.

John Colenso was a tall, upstanding man with a good presence, a good horseman, and the normal propensities of an entirely, but exclusively, masculine nature. Frances Bunyon was the woman for him: two years younger, well educated and well read, with a wider culture than his. While he was still enclosed in the grim treadmill of his Evangelical upbringing, she had read Coleridge, knew the Kingsleys, and introduced Colenso to the modernism— more open-minded, if somewhat muddled—of Frederic Denison Maurice.

In private, beneath the stoical endurance that left its imprint upon his features, Colenso always had a certain winning charm— there are testimonies to it from many different sources. He was warm-hearted and generous; one finds him taking an orphan girl under his wing and, when financial trouble struck the Bunyons, he at once offered to arrange for them lodgings in Cambridge. Naif as always, he was amazed at their refusing the offer.

The fact was that for some years he and Frances could not marry: there was no money. Until a good College living fell in, at Forncett St Mary in Norfolk; then they were free to marry, and incontinently did, at Hawksmoor's church of St George's, Bloomsbury.

The couple remained in Norfolk for the seven years, 1846-1853. There four of their five children were born. They threw themselves into parish work, both teaching in the village, he preaching about in the neighbourhood, taking on more pupils from Cambridge, writing more textbooks, a chore to reduce his debts and help others—notably the education of his brother.

All this was not enough: Colenso longed for work in the mission field and the freedom of spirit it would give. He took on the work of organising secretary locally for the S.P.G., Society for the Propagation of the Gospel; he preached for the Church Missionary Society, and edited two of the S.P.G.'s journals, *The Church in the Colonies* and *The Monthly Record*. When his brother-in-law went out to Borneo as Bishop of Labuan, Colenso was sad that his burden of debt kept him tied at home.

Suddenly the burden was lifted. Longmans offered to buy the copyright of his text-books outright for some £2400, the sum to which he had reduced his debt by hard work. Colenso accepted—to be free at last. I fear that it was not very businesslike of him: he should have held on to his copyright, and that would have made him eventually independent. In the Victorian age Longmans—leading among publishers and oldest among them—had two famous authors who held out for every ha'penny of their royalties. I forget who the first was, but the second was John Henry Newman. Colenso did not make a good bargain for himself, but he was free at last. For a spirit so independent, so bent on fulfilling himself in the work he had long had in mind, this was everything.

At that moment Robert Gray, bishop of Capetown, was in England looking for a recruit to undertake part of the burden of his enormous diocese, as bishop of Natal. The two men, who were to become such opponents, took a liking to each other, and Gray signed Colenso on for the job. Apparently without time to consider what Gray might have regarded as danger signals, if he had thought about it. For Gray was a High Churchman, no intellectual and completely conventional in his beliefs; Colenso's background was Low Church, but he had progressed along with F.D. Maurice to what became known as Modernism.

Maurice did not believe in the doctrine of Eternal Punishment—that the great bulk of mankind (except for a few elect persons, notably those most strongly addicted to the doctrine—for others) would be consigned in the hereafter to endless torment for sin. (Nor, for that matter, had the enlightened Archbishop Laud, who objected to the Puritan Lord Saye-and-Sele that his soul revolted from such doctrine—the essence of Calvinist Predestination.)

Maurice was ejected from his professorship at King's College, London, for his inability to subscribe to this nonsense. At this moment Colenso had his *Village Sermons* ready for the press; he at once dedicated the book to the man under sentence. It was courageous of him—he was always fearless; one must not say without thought of consequences, for though quick in his reactions and by nature quick-tempered, he knew perfectly well what he was doing. He now openly aligned himself with Maurice against the wicked nonsense of eternal damnation.[1] He regarded it as 'utterly contrary to the whole spirit of the Gospel—as obscuring the Grace of God and perverting His Message of Love and "Goodwill to Man"; and operating, with most injurious and deadening effect, both on those who teach and those who are taught.'

He never minced his words; he realised that this doctrine of misery was of most deadening and injurious effect precisely among the unconverted in the mission field. For them a stumbling block, for the orthodox and conventional his rejection of it was a danger signal.

1. For a specimen here is what Dr Pusey, leader of the Oxford Movement after Newman's defection to Rome, enforced in a University Sermon: 'Gather in your mind all which is most loathsome, most revolting, the most treacherous, malicious, coarse, brutal, inventive, fiendish cruelty, unsoftened by any remains of human feeling; conceive the fierce, fiery eyes of hate, spite, frenzied rage ever fixed on thee, glaring eyes on thee, looking thee through and through with hate, sleepless in their horrible gaze. Hear those yells of blasphemous concentrated hate as they echo along the lurid vaults of Hell, everyone hating everyone.' What an ass! the sainted Doctor must just have had a diseased imagination.

Chapter III
Natal

Colenso sailed from Plymouth, in company with the bishop of Capetown and his spouse, on 15 December 1853, on a tour of inspection of Natal to see how the land lay and to report back home. His report was most favourable as to prospects and is enshrined in his attractive book, soon written, *Ten Weeks in Natal.* It is entirely characteristic of the man: factual and literal, all following orderly method, it yet has a certain charm. For he at once fell in love with the beauty of the country, several times comparing scenes to those in Devon and Cornwall; 'I am often reminded of my native Cornish hills, except that here the proportions of the scenery are much more gigantic.'

In those ten weeks, with his usual energy, he covered the original Natal, then only about one-third of England and Wales. He calculated the population as some 6000 Europeans, of whom 1000 were Dutch, and 100,000 to 120,000 blacks. He found the blacks friendly to the British, not so to the Boers. The Boers adhered religiously to Old Testament ideas of slavery, as did the whites contemporaneously in the Southern States of USA. We must in fairness remember that blacks enslaved each other with equal alacrity. It was the British who had renounced slavery and ended the slave-trade, while the sainted Puritans of New England—the Baptists of Rhode island, for example—continued it. In the century-long struggle between British and Boers in South Africa, there was always this underlying issue: the Boers believed in slavery, the British did not.

An historian may venture the opinion that, if the British had been dominant in South Africa, there never would have been *apartheid.*[1] Race relations would have produced conflict and

1. cf. B. Bunting, *The Rise of the South African Reich*, 19. 'There was a fundamental difference over the treatment of the non-Whites. The British since 1854 had had a constitution overtly without colour bar in the Cape, and their attitudes were projected northwards immediately after the [Boer] War.'

difficulty as always, but it would not have been a clear-cut conflict on ideological grounds. The British are not given to ideology, but are empirical and pragmatic: there would have been continual compromises and concessions, not direct confrontation. It is probable that solutions would have been gradually worked out, shifting and imprecise, but tolerable. This was the issue at the back of the conflict between British and Boers, and why the latter trekked away from British rule to the interior where they could do what they liked—and did.

On the other hand, an American historian reminds us that the Boers were not colonials, they were indigenous.[1] They were in South Africa for more than a century before they encountered a solid native population moving south into the empty spaces of South Africa, which the Boers regarded—as they still do—as *their* country.

In the earlier decades of the 19th century Natal itself had been largely emptied by the appalling ravages of the great Zulu empire-builder, Chaka. The Zulus had originally been a small tribe among others, but more predatory—as our American authority points out—they no more considered other ethnic blacks, particularly Bushmen and Hottentots, than the Boers did. They were even more ruthless, and Chaka a monster of savagery—and ability. He conquered and massacred black peoples in every direction, broke up their tribes, took possession of their lands, and annexed the remnants of broken peoples to his dominant Zulus. He built up and organised a powerful army, even regimented and disciplined it; his young braves were not allowed to marry until they had 'washed their spears' in blood, no matter whose.

Chaka eventually got his comeuppance in the usual way; but he left his royal house to succeed him, he left his memory— which Colenso found the Zulus still venerating, his grave kept secret and sacred; above all he left his army, some 30,000 young braves organized and bent on 'washing their spears'. This independent Zulu kingdom north of Natal, beyond the Tugela and stretching up to the Drakensberg border with the

---

1. Donald R. Morris, *The Washing of the Spears. The Rise and Fall of the Zulu Nation.*

Transvaal, was a factor of prime importance henceforth in South Africa, under Chaka's successors. The Zulus were militant, and militarist; they could not but be a threat to their neighbours—and fear often sparks off war.

Colenso was not starry-eyed about the Zulus, for all that he came to the defence of their later King, Cetewayo, when he was treated with manifest injustice. Colenso was informed of Chaka's record from earlier inhabitants of Natal; his successor Dingaan continued Chaka's pretty little ways. Only some fifteen years before Colenso's visit Dingaan had exterminated the Dutch Mission in his country: in February 1838 'Dutch Boers to the number of 70, besides many of their children and Hottentot servants [Colenso would never allow 'slaves'] were savagely butchered in cold blood by the orders of the king.' Then followed the massacre of Piet Retief and his whole party, 'encamped near to the present township of Weenen (*weeping*), which derives its name from the sad events of that day. The prime warriors of this camp having been already slain, those who remained behind were easily overpowered. Men, women, and children were surrounded and mercilessly butchered.' Zulu detachments surprised other camps of settlers, until the spreading alarm gave time for the Dutch farmers to collect themselves within *laagers*, the one effective technique of resistance.

Chaka's ways with his own people were no better–if anything worse, in keeping with custom and religion. On his mother's death, 'ten of the best-looking girls of the kraal'—it was reported to Colenso—'being buried alive'. During the prolonged funeral ceremonies, with lamentations—that remind one of American Indian customs as reported by the Elizabethans—proclamation of sacrifices was made: 'no cultivation should be allowed during the following year; no milk should be used, but it should be all poured upon the earth; and all women who should be found with child during the year should with their husbands be put to death. . . The next morning the Purification took place. Every cattle-owner had brought calves for this purpose, each of which was ripped open on its right side, the owner taking out the gall of the living animal, which then was left to die in its agonies, and not allowed to be eaten. Each regiment in succession then presented itself before Chaka, each individual holding the gall-bladder in his hand, sprinkled the gall over him.'

It is not to be supposed that the animal sacrifices of the Old Testament—they had been transmuted from human sacrifice—were essentially any different; the courts of the Temple, 'all glorious within', were slaughter-houses, the priests killers. But today—are slaughter-houses any better? We avert our minds from the suffering of the animals we live on and off. 'Nature, red in tooth and claw' – the whole fabric of life from top to bottom feeds one upon the other.

Colenso had not had the advantage of a course in anthropology, an only recently developing subject of study, but he writes commonsense about native polygamy. (Anyway, weren't the whites up to it contemporaneously in the New Zion, Utah?) 'I must confess that I feel very strongly on this point, that the usual practice of enforcing the separation of wives from their husbands, upon their conversion to Christianity, is quite unwarrantable, and opposed to the teaching of our Lord. It is putting new wine into old bottles, and placing a stumbling-block, which He has not set, directly in the way of their receiving the Gospel. . . What is to become of their children? Who is to have the care of them?' What about Abraham and other Old Testament worthies? 'What is the use of our reading to them the Bible stories of Abraham, Israel, and David with their many wives?'

This at once became a rock of offence for the good Bishop with the orthodox in England—no imagination, no sense of other circumstances than their own; in short, no sense. One glimpses the practical difficulties the Bishop would shortly be up against, the moment he took up his burden.

Nor had Colenso the advantage of our academic fascination with the subject of witchcraft. The blacks were obsessed with, ruled by, witchcraft. Even under the less inhuman régime of Cetewayo an accusation of witchcraft meant death. Wizards were both doctors and priests to the natives. Oddly enough, when the son of a leading white official in the colony fell ill, Cetewayo sent him his personal witch-doctor—and the boy recovered. I suppose the boy would have recovered anyway; it reminds one of Rasputin and the Tsarevitch.

Colenso would hardly have known of the witch-mania unleashed in the Europe of the 16th and 17th centuries, at its height in England under the rule of the Puritans. No such cruel nonsense from cultivated spirits like Charles I and Archbishop Laud, good Anglicans who actively discouraged preposterous Calvinism. (James I, theologically Calvinist, was obsessed with demonology.) Colenso found the blacks reluctant to kill snakes on account of their belief that the spirits return in the form of snakes. (It is men's beliefs that make fools of them.) Before Isandhlwana one officer, bitten by a black mamba, died next day—no-one has ever been known to recover from the bite of that one of God's creatures.

The Bishop found that there was not a single hospital in the Colony, which had been taken over by the British only a few years before. He at once planned one, to take shape along with the mission stations he projected; four of these eventually came into being, along with another over the border in Zululand. He was to found churches and schools. More personally, he selected a beautiful site for his Bishopstowe, within view of a splendid Table mountain; there was to be his home, and alongside of that a special school for the instruction of Zulus.

He made friends with Theophilus Shepstone, the remarkable man who was in charge of native affairs. Shepstone was the son of a Wesleyan missionary, so he and the Bishop had something of the great Wesley in common in their background: 'the world is my parish.' Shepstone was a good linguist, with a full knowledge of Zulu and the Zulu mentality. This gave him a commanding influence with the blacks, and his policy had the confidence of the government at home.

It was a paternalist one, properly suited to the conditions obtaining, and generous in its intentions. Many refugees had streamed into Natal from Chaka's rule, and Shepstone set aside large areas for native reserves. This was not in keeping with the ideas of either Boers or British: the former wanted slaves, the latter a free labour market of blacks for their wants.

Thus Shepstone was not popular with the colonists, but

he and Colenso became firm friends—'my dearest friend', Colenso called him. For twenty years they worked together, the administrator giving the Bishop what support he could in the latter's constructive work. One must remember, however, that the Bishop was an independent power, with Church funds for his work and his own lines of communication with the government at home, the Colonial Office and with public opinion in England.

Shepstone had his own sphere of influence with the blacks, with whom he too took a moral line, weaning them away from savagery and advising them for their good. This line had its limitations. After one of his moral lectures to a tribe, what the chief said at the end of it was, 'How do you make gunpowder?' Rider Haggard, who had a farm in South Africa and lived there for several years, expresses the view that missionaries had no permanent effect on the black mentality at all.[1]

This, though more realistic than Colenso's, appears too cynical a view. Christian preaching and teaching were at least directed towards peaceful ends, trying to stop the natives from killing one another—in Africa as eventually in New Zealand. Such at last was the constant teaching and preaching of the missionaries.

From the first Colenso appreciated Shepstone and his work. His father was still working away as a Wesleyan missionary among the Hottentots in the Northern Cape Colony. The son had become a Churchman, and as churchwarden was a pillar of the church at Pietermaritzburg, which the Bishop was to preside over. When Colenso came in from Bishopstowe, some eight miles out, for Sunday service he spent an hour with Shepstone beforehand. Already he compared him with the famous west countryman, Rajah Brooke of Sarawak.

On his tour Colenso held confirmations, something new for colonists and natives alike. It fell to him to bury Dr Stranger, who had made a name on one of the Niger expeditions. It was

---

1. cf. H. Rider Haggard, *Cetywayo and his White Neighbours.* He has been condemned as an 'imperialist', but it is worth noting that he considered that the British had treated the Boers unjustly. Similarly the 'imperialist' historian Froude favoured the Boers against the British colonists, cf my *Froude, the Historian.*

not long before that the intrepid young Cornishman, Richard Lander, had discovered the source of the Niger, hitherto a remarkable mystery of the Dark Continent. Lander gave his life to his enthusiasm as explorer: today one sees his memorial in the tall column at the top of Lemon Street in his native Truro. At Maritzburg Colenso found two more Wesleyan missionaries at work, both from Cornwall, one a St Austell man, he noted.

On his return he toured round the country collecting contributions for the good work, preaching and holding meetings. Harrow was foremost in the support it gave him, and raised most money – a tribute to him, it showed he had not been forgotten there. Cambridge followed suit. Nor was Cornwall behindhand: sermons in the three churches of Truro followed by a meeting; similarly in St Austell; sermons at Bodmin, Lostwithiel and Helston; small sums from women friends—one recognises the names, St Aubyn, Trevelyan, Pendarves, Rodd, Mrs Foster of Lostwithiel.

Altogether, with the proceeds from his book, he raised £11,000—a considerable sum, after much effort; one should multiply by perhaps a hundred today, in the deplorable decline of sterling, for contemporary valuation. Shepstone entirely approved the Bishop's plans for his work—he himself was full of hope. Other workers, missionaries and teachers, would find 'the Bishop, with his family at hand, to welcome, to counsel, and to comfort them with spiritual advice and daily ministrations of God's Word. Here too they will be able to "consider one another, and to provoke unto love and good works".' All rather pathetic when one considers the sequel—and the provocation that ensued was of a very different kind.

For the seven years 1854–1861 Colenso worked away at his primary task as missionary bishop. We need not go into the wearisome round of episcopal duties—preaching most Sundays in his cathedral, ordinations and confirmations, which the intellectual Bishop Creighton used to describe as 'setting in with their usual severity', as if measles or chicken pox. Colenso had more than the usual difficulties with his clergy, an unsatisfactory lot—difficult to recruit better. The Dean of his cathedral, one Green, was very unco-operative; a High Churchman, he kept a constant look-out for heresy in the Bishop's sermons, and eventually delated him to the Bishop of Cape Town for heresy.

This foreshadowed the later tangle of troubles. The bishop of Cape Town had no legal authority over the bishop of Natal, merely shadowy claims to spiritual jurisdiction as Metropolitan. When Colenso was eventually cited before Gray for heresy, he took no notice. He had his own views of Gray's intellectual inferiority—who never claimed, conventional High Churchman that he was, to be much of a thinker. Intellectually Colenso was formidably equipped—more so than the whole bench of bishops in England, except Tait and Thirlwall. He was very sure of himself in this field, a fast worker, quick to reach conclusions, not one to suffer fools gladly, and irritated with obstinate refusal to see sense, so common a feature with ordinary minds. Not very tolerant of opposition, his wife thought.

His was obviously not an ordinary mind – the amount of work he got through in those seven years, in learning Zulu and translating into it, was enough for one man's life's work. Colenso cleared the way through the intricacies of Zulu grammar, with the first-class mind of a Cambridge classic— the Cambridge school used to be described as 'high and dry', as against the less accurate, more humanistic, approach of a Jowett at Oxford. Colenso's *First Steps in Zulu* became the standard Grammar, and I learn that the system of orthography which he worked out was that adhered to subsequently —a sufficient claim to fame, or at least remembrance, in itself.

The book is a model of its kind in method, order, making things as simple and clear as may be: a mirror of Colenso's own mind. 'The Zulu-Kafir language is properly the dialect of a small tribe, the amaZulu, who under their famous chief Chaka and his brothers and successors, Dingane and Mpande have acquired and maintained, for some sixty years, the supremacy over the natives along the S-E. coast of Africa—excepting of course those who have been living under British protection since Natal came under our Government in 1845. On this account it has a right to be considered the standard dialect of this part of Africa, though other varieties of the kafir language are spoken by different tribes within, and far beyond, the borders of the Colony.

'At the present time the district of Natal is largely occupied by a very mixed population of native tribes. The majority of them are sprung from the aboriginal inhabitants, who either took refuge in the natural fastnesses of the country when the desolating waves of Chaka's invasions rolled over the land, or had fled beyond his reach into the neighbouring districts ... Others have since come in from all quarters round to seek shelter and protection under a civilised government.'

Though it is not the thing to say so, I should have thought that the poor souls were better off there than under Chaka's terror. Colenso chose the dominant dialect, which is 'intelligible to any Zulu and may be heard at the royal Kraal. Indeed Mpande's great wife, now a refugee in this colony, uses it habitually, though her son Mkungo does not, but speaks the pure Zulu.' Colenso knew these distinctions; for the boy princeling Mkungo was, with Shepstone's approval, taken into the school at Bishopstowe to be brought up. In his native Zululand his life was as much in danger from his loving relatives as the Princes in the Tower were from their uncle, Richard III. (Humans have nasty ways, whatever their colour.) The intrepid Bishop made a journey across the border into Zululand, to plant a mission station; so that, one way and another, Shepstone involved him in its politics. But his knowledge of the language was intimate from his daily life and surroundings, not only the school, where his daughters taught; they too, both Harriet and Frances Ellen, were fluent in the language.

Among the scholars was an intelligent youth, William Ngidi, who became a great help. He had a way of putting searching questions, which obliged the conscientious Colenso, honest man, to think out anew the answers they demanded. In England, when the rumpus about Colenso's *Pentateuch* broke out, Ngidi was caricatured as 'the Intelligent Zulu' – as if the critical treatment the Old Testament demanded (and was receiving in Germany) depended on that simple source. The youth's questions, however, did go to the heart of the matter. While the Bishop was away in England, William read St Paul for himself and noted the expectation on the part of Jesus' disciples of his imminent return—and his non-appearance. How to account for that? Could they all have been wrong about him? Here was a typical poser.

Disraeli dismissed a lot of the fuss with his sensible cynicism – he wasn't burning his fingers by taking it seriously: 'Remarkable people, the Zulus! They defeat our generals [at Isandhlwana]; they convert our bishops [Colenso]; they bring to an end a great European dynasty' [the killing of the Prince Imperial, Napoleon III's heir, on campaign there].

And so to the language, the characteristic Zulu clicks, described by Colenso with his usual factual precision. 'The letters *c*, *q*, *x*, are taken to represent the *clicks*, which are sounds not heard in any European language, being used to denote the *dental, palatal,* and *lateral* clicks respectively, so called from their being uttered by thrusting the tongue against the *top of the front teeth,* the *roof of the mouth,* and the *side-teeth,* and suddenly withdrawing it.' What description could be clearer, or more precise?

And so on to rhyme, rhythm, and accentuation. 'The Kafir Language is very ill adapted for the composition of hymns in *rhyme.* . . Again, the regular fall of the accent on the penulti-mate makes the ordinary Long, Common, and Short Metres of English Psalmody utterly unsuitable for Zulu hymns. These tunes should on no account be used for this purpose. The practice of doing so arises from want of due considera-tion, or else from mere want of taste. Missionaries too often compel the natives to offend against all the laws of accen-tuation, and force the rhythm of their own words constantly in singing, in order to accommodate our favourite tunes. Let any Englishman attempt to sing the line 'O'er the gloomy hills of darkness' to any L.M. or C.M. tune, and he will soon be convinced of the frightful effect which the singing of words to such tunes must have upon the ear of the natives.' Such a detail is rather unexpected from him, one wouldn't have thought that he had a musical ear, but one sees again his overriding consideration for the native. Now, 'for prose hymns suited for chanting, like the Psalms, or for *metrical* hymns *without rhyme*, the Zulu language is very well adapted.'

We will not venture with him into the complexities of Zulu grammar, the peculiarities of construction, the special use of the verb 'ti', etc, it is amusing enough to see the conditions of native life reflected in the examples. '*Uba asibute uTshaka*, when Chaka mustered us; *ube sibuye empini*, when we returned from the fight; *bati ukufika kwabo, bambamba, bamtshaya*, they, at their arrival, seized him and beat him.' It would be a Philistine comment, unworthy of Colenso, to say that it reminds one of the rigmarole that Shakespeare invented to decoy Parolles in *All's Well That Ends Well*.

Colenso followed this up with a whole programme of books to compass the education of the natives – experienced as he was in providing text-books at home. A *First, Second,* and *Third Reading Book* provided tales and stories; then a *précis* of geography and history, followed by *First Lessons in Science*, and *Umzimba Ozwayo, (The Living Body)*, *First Lessons in Physiology*. This secular programme was ultimately topped by a *Zulu-English Dictionary*, giving the meanings of some 64,000 words.

On the religious side—though Colenso would have made no rigid distinction, it was all good works to him—he translated the whole of the New Testament into Zulu, most of the Prayer Book with many of the Psalms (he would have omitted the vengeful and comminatory ones); from the Old Testament the Books of Genesis, Exodus, and Samuel; and characteristically the First Part of Bunnion's[1] *Pilgrim's Progress*. More amusingly, he published *Three Native Accounts* of his own Journey into Zululand, with translations and notes, perhaps *pour encourager les autres*.

But what a prodigious work for one man to have accomplished, unaided—and it was only one side of his activities!

We have to consider the effect of his missionary work on himself, and ultimately in South Africa. 'To teach the truths of our holy religion to intelligent adult natives, who have the simplicity of children but withal the earnestness and thoughtfulness of men—whose minds are not prepared by long familiarity to acquiesce in if not to receive them—is a sifting

---

1. Evidently the derivation of the name Bunyan.

process for any teacher who feels the deep moral obligations of answering truly, and faithfully, and unreservedly, his fellow man looking up to him for light and guidance and asking— "Are you sure of this?" "Do you believe this?" "Do you believe that?" '

Here we come to the essence of Colenso's mind—his utter honesty and his courage in facing up to what he did believe, *sifting* his own mind. Any historian, if he is any good, knows that ordinary humans at all times and in all places will believe any nonsense—and kill each other for not believing it. They accept what they have been brought up in without thinking about it—naturally enough, for they are incapable of *thinking*, strictly speaking, and never will be capable. (So what price their education?—a very limited affair, largely practical.) But there are certain elect minds for whom it is not sufficient to accept the nonsense everybody else accepts, but are impelled to think what is really true amid the mental rubbish that lumbers the average mind. Colenso was one of these uncomfortable few.

There are, of course, clever sceptics—some of them Popes, like Leo X who thought Christianity a 'profitable superstition'—who keep their thoughts to themselves, and do not impart them to the dear people. Colenso was not one of those: he was not a sceptic. He was a genuine believer who was prepared to teach others only what he really believed himself. He was prepared to sift himself, and then to speak out.

'The state of everlasting torment after death—of all impenitent sinners and unbelievers, including the whole heathen world—as many teach—is naturally so amazing and overwhelming an object of contemplation to them and one so prominently put forward in the case of those who have been under certain Missionary training, that it quite shuts out the cardinal doctrines of the Gospel, the Fatherly relation to us of the Faithful Creator.'

He had earlier accepted the doctrine of eternal punishment, like everybody else, without thinking about it. Of course it had had tremendous utility in keeping order in the nursery, keeping the masses on the rails. In our day, with the breakdown of religious belief, we feel the want of it, and some of the consequences in the irresponsible, and worse, conduct of people at large who have no inner *rationale* to control themselves—external controls having everywhere broken down. Except possibly in communist countries, though even there their positivist dogma is no longer believed in by the intelligent.

Colenso found that the preaching of eternal punishment by missionaries held the natives back from conversion— they were revolted by it. And when he himself looked into it he had to face the fact that it was nonsense—instead of what he really did believe in, 'the common ground of our humanity.'

So what was he left with to teach his flock, blacks and whites alike? He preached only the Lord's Prayer and the Sermon on the Mount. To reduce Christian doctrine to this undogmatic position was heresy to Victorian orthodoxy. There is sense in Chesterton's old joke: 'Orthodoxy is my doxy, heterodoxy is other people's doxy.' Intelligent persons never accept other people's nonsense unexamined, and only the elect 'speak out loud'—as I have heard it put in USA—about it. Colenso was one of those; but also he was forced to speak out from his position in the mission field.

He was now to discover, for all his efforts, not only the inadequacy but the inefficacy of most missionary work. 'The great drawback here is that the country is already saturated with a corruption of Christianity, and the natives have acquired such a view of the character of God and of the Gospel as keeps them back from desiring to have a much closer acquaintance with it.'

This led him on to give thought anew to the foundations of New Testament teaching in the Old Testament, and to lay bare the barbarisms and superstitions of the ancient Hebrews—obvious enough to reflective natives, who recognised the similarity with their own.

An authoritative observer from within South Africa sums up: 'by the early 1860's John Colenso, Bishop of Natal, had come to the conclusion that there were serious weaknesses in the whole structure of mission life and missionary teaching. These weaknesses made it impossible for those with a genuine concern for the spread of Christianity to do their work honestly and effectively.'[1]

And the further conclusion is reached, of lasting importance and relevant today: 'but Colenso's arguments were rejected then, and they have been ignored ever since.'

We shall see that Colenso's argments—still more, his advice and example—were rejected also in a far more important field: that of race relations in South Africa—with the apalling consequences we see there today. What *bloody* idiots humans are!

Our South African authority concludes, 'it was not that Colenso was unable to understand that economic and ideological change is inextricably interrelated—indeed he stressed that industrial training and changes in the standards of material life were intrinsic to Christian teaching. It was that he believed that such changes could be brought about by persuasion, effective communication, devotion and hard work: to believe this is all that is needed is to fail to understand that struggle between irreconcilable forces is the dynamic of historical change.'

In plainer language, what this means is that Colenso's task was ultimately impossible. Himself was not only an idealist but an optimist. De Gaulle: '*Pour agir il faut espérer.*' But to what end?

However, Colenso left a legacy in South Africa, not only in his ideals but in good works—in his linguistic work and in politics, if not in the numinous and nebulous realm of religion.

---

1. Jeff Guy: *The Heretic. A Study of the Life of John William Colenso*, 78–82.

Chapter IV

The Bible and Belief

From 1860 a new wind was blowing to shake Victorians out of their comfortable orthodoxy. Here we must notice a significant fact not often realised. The 19th century had reacted against 18th century Rationalism, when a Georgian bishop, Watson, could say of the Creeds that, after all, they were 'all of human fabrication.' The reaction was a European phenomenon, just as noticeable in France: the critical Rationalism of the Enlightenment, such unbelieving spirits as Voltaire and Diderot, had prepared the ground for the French Revolution. In the reaction from its horrors the upper classes everywhere closed ranks. Orthodoxy regained strength, all the more so because one can detect the positive fear behind the front, the sense of insecurity at its being challenged—one stone loosened might precipitate the avalanche.

Colenso was not an upper-class man. Moreover, he was not even English, and had not the English gift for humbug: he was a Cornish Celt, with the disadvantages (and advantages) of the Celtic temperament. The unconscious elements in a man's make-up are more important than superficial observers realise, and the marked sympathies of both Colensos with the underdogs, Zulu and Maori, owe more than they themselves realised to their own exceptional backgrounds.

In 1859 Darwin at last produced his *Origin of Species* with its shattering revelation that the innumerable species of life on the planet had not been produced all at one time by the benevolent Creator, black mambas and all; and with its revolutionary suggestion of the antiquity of man over a long process of evolution. At the same time the foremost geologist, Lyell, revealed the hardly less disturbing fact of the age of the earth, the aeons of time the rocks, the geological facts, revealed. Even the leading Oxford geologist before him, Professor Buckland, who could swallow the heart of Louis

XVI,[1] could not swallow the facts of geology.

Then a few intelligent clerics of the younger generation tried to come to terms with the new knowledge flooding in, with their *Essays and Reviews*. This harmless book created grave scandal and continuing trouble for the careers of its clerical authors. There was public protest at one of them, Frederick Temple, being made later bishop of Exeter. The sainted Pusey, who failed to get another, Jowett of Balliol, out of his professorship of Greek at least managed to get his stipend stopped. Jowett ceased to burn his fingers with the Interpretation of Holy Scripture and concentrated henceforth on translating Plato. Here also not altogether blamelessly—see J.A. Symonds' strictures upon him for ignoring the patent homosexual implications of the text. Really, the *unawareness* of the Victorians is hardly credible.

The Victorians were in fact persecutors. Frederic Denison Maurice was forced to resign from King's College, London, for not toeing the line of orthodox belief. A really eminent scholar, Robertson Smith, was dismissed from Aberdeen for writing historical sense about the Old Testament. Samuel Davidson was sacked from his Lancashire Independent College for his commonsense about the Bible. Then there was Heath, and others; very superior intelligences, like Leslie Stephen at Cambridge, and J. A. Froude at Oxford, dropped their deacons' orders and moved out of the minefield, though not without a rumpus.

On top of all this came Colenso – and he a bishop!

There was in fact no biblical criticism worthy of the name in England, which was far behind Germany in classical and historical scholarship as well. Moreover, few English scholars knew German—apparently Pusey did, but with him time had stopped, somewhere around 1833. In Germany there was a welter of writing about the Bible; one body of conservative

---

1. Professor Buckland, who had the odd habit of swallowing whatever he fancied, was dining at Nuneham Courtenay one night when Louis XVI's dried heart, preserved in a little box, was passed round the table for inspection as a curiosity. The Professor incontinently swallowed it, to the disgust of his hosts, the Harcourts. Buckland was no fool, but a bit of an eccentric; he was in fact the most distinguised geologist in England, before Lyell, who began as his pupil.

scholars tried, disingenuously, to make sense of the incon-
sistencies of the narratives and to explain away their contradictions. The newer school, the 'Higher Criticism', brought
them into the light of day.

Colenso had then to learn German, and thereupon did. He
was entirely on his own—really a lonely soul, except for his
understanding wife—but he was formidably equipped. A good
classical scholar who was also a mathematician, he was
confident of his Hebrew, which he had begun to study in his
schooldays—as he explained to a bishop who tried answering
him, while modestly admitting that *he* knew neither Hebrew
nor German.

Without Victorian religious prejudice we can appreciate
much better, at its true value, the remarkable Hebrew literature of the Old Testament. It is indeed 'an unparalleled
compilation',[1] perhaps the finest of ancient literatures, except
for Greek. And, though Greek literature is more varied and
genial, the Hebrew of the Old Testament is more concentrated
and powerful, and by this fact makes greater impact. Where
the Greek genius was aesthetic and philosophic, seeking
moderation and proportion, the Hebrew was moral and religious, with a passionate seeking for purity in all things. The Old
Testament, because of its passion, speaks more directly to us
all, and to the soul.

But it *has* variety. Along with much myth and folklore,
poetry and prophetic denunciation, there is a great deal of
ancient history, some of it older than Herodotus and Thucy-
dides. As historical writing, much is unique, among the
earliest in civilisation, and of the utmost value to the historian.

Of course it needs critical elucidation; of course the reliable
history needs disentangling from myth and fable, popular
imaginings about the past, the particular bias of one writer as
against another—for example, a northern historian of Israel,
as against the southern record of Judah. Moreover, the compilation contains layer upon layer, some of it very early, some of
it much later; and it has been edited and re-edited, with
insertions into earlier texts made at different times.

So that it is a highly expert business to clarify different

1. Michael Grant: *A History of Ancient Israel*, 1.

strands, demanding as much expertise as Homeric scholarship, perhaps even more. The process of scholarly
clarification—as with Homer or Shakespeare—leads to a
clearer and richer understanding of the subject.

One would have thought that people would be grateful (if
one did not know what fools they are) for a great scholar, an
incisive mind, like Colenso initiating the process of clarifying
the Old Testament for our benefit. For all effective purposes,
in Britain he was the beginner, cutting a path through the
undergrowth of centuries, blazing a trail through the fog, the
miasma of misunderstanding, prejudice and ignorance.

So far from people being grateful, so far from their feeding
on what he gave them in their hearts with thanksgiving, he was
traduced and abused, constantly misrepresented and misunderstood—when usually no effort was made to understand
him by ordinary stupids and, worse, by a lot of superior people
who should have known better. (We shall see an example of
misunderstanding in such quarters even today.)

Of course, he had his supporters—practically all the major
scientists of the day, many of the best writers, and even the
more enlightened intellects among the clergy, though few—
such men as Jowett and Dean Stanley.

Altogether it makes a singular story—with a moral.

Colenso began by examining the conservative German
scholars and showing up the unsatisfactory character of their
attempts to make out that all was well. There was no English
work in the field worth considering to answer. He worked
prodigiously fast, producing thick volumes *coup sur coup* until
his total work on the Pentateuch—the first five books of the
Old Testament—reached seven Parts. (He called his horse
that carried him about his diocese 'Pentateuch', with some
relaxation into humour; once Pentateuch plunged him into a
flood. With his unsuperstitious mind the good Bishop did not
take it as an ill omen.) The Victorian printers kept pace with
him through the early 1860's—tribute to the efficiency and
care of *Victorian* printing.

As one reads the First Part of the big book one cannot but
note Colenso's excitement at his discoveries, even something
like high spirits. It was all new and disturbing to him. Hitherto

he had accepted the conventional view of it all without devoting thought to it; now that he went into the subject for himself, he made any number of discoveries. He had had no forerunners. Wasn't that sufficiently exciting in itself?—So far from people being grateful at having the problems of Holy Writ cleared up for them, they were infuriated.

Colenso was not entirely without tact: he did *not* at once say all that was in his mind. His method was very much that of the 'high and dry' Cambridge school, literal and factual analysis, sentence by sentence, statement by statement, of the first five Sacred Books. But the total effect was devastating—and unanswerable. It is astonishing how much of his critical work stands. We must allow that the way was wide-open, the opportunity there for the asking, much of it today appearing obvious common sense. This in itself is evidence how little sensible work had been done in the field, with the tabu upon it.

Today modern scholarship largely corroborates Colenso's findings—working entirely on his own in his study in faraway Natal, crammed with books, no-one whom he could consult, no-one to help him. That may have been an advantage—it fortified his concentration and independence of mind. Our leading authority today writes of his work on the beginning of Genesis, 'by pointing out the two sources separately, following on from the detailed analysis, Colenso enables us to see easily how close his results were to the commonly accepted modern source-division of Genesis I-II. . . Colenso seems to have been such an independent person that it is unlikely that he did not weigh every consideration very carefully before reaching his conclusions.'[1]

Professor Rogerson pays tribute to the conscientious scrupulousness of the work – in keeping with what we know to be the dominant character of the man, *honesty*. 'But it has to be admitted that he does his work devastatingly. He is at his most brilliantly destructive in discussing the Flood. He pictures how the Ark was inhabited: with snails and insects as well as animals and birds. He estimates how many sheep there must have been to satisfy the carnivores for over a year, in addition to the sheep meant to be preserved. He imagines the drudgery

1. Rogerson, 225–6.

of the daily routine of Noah and his family, feeding all these animals, birds and other creatures [black mambas?], renewing their litter and disposing of their excrement. He wonders how some insects got on which do not normally live in pairs, the bees for example. He ponders the difficulties of temperature. Not only would the Ark contain animals from hot climates, but reindeer would be there too. And when the Ark finally grounded on Mt. Ararat, 17,000 feet above sea level, it would have been very cold indeed in the Ark.'

Colenso must have got some fun out of this nonsense—and deserved to for all the homework he put in in those solitary hours at Bishopstowe. But it was no laughing matter to the humbugs at home. The heavy Lightfoot, regarded as a great theologian, gives detailed measurements of what the Ark must have been. One day in Victorian London there was a particularly heavy fog; Dean Church up at St Paul's said that Lightfoot down at Westminster must have gone to bed leaving his bedroom window open—the fog had spread all over London. Bishop Harold Browne, who graduated from Ely to the fat see of Winchester with Farnham Castle to live in, opined that Noah took with him into the Ark all the insects, with their eggs and larvae. (Bishop Browne fancied himself for archbishop of Canterbury; it took Queen Victoria herself to tell him that he was too old for the job.) Another clerical ass put forward the view that, if one dug beneath the snows of Mount Ararat, the Ark would be found.

Silly as those pomposities were, there are still plenty of people in the less enlightened parts of USA who hold fast to these absurdities—or even in England, among the sects (rather than insects). A colleague at All Souls once tuned in to one of their orators in Hyde Park. A voice in the audience put forward the objection that, of some 60,000 different species how could there be room in the Ark? The preacher found no objection. Another objector grumbled, 'How about the great carnivores?' No notice was taken.

Bishop Wilberforce of Oxford, 'Soapy Sam', took the lead in the campaign against Bishop Colenso. On arriving in England Colenso received a letter from Bishop Wilberforce which illustrates the appropriateness of the latter's soubriquet. 'I should greatly like calmly and *prayerfully* to talk with you, if you will let me' Soapy Sam was no scholar, but an adept ecclesi-astical politician.[1] Colenso found that, instead of a prayerful discussion, he was to be convened for judgment. Wilberforce took the lead among the bishops. Colenso's name was dropped from the S.P.G. (Society for the Propagation of the Gospel), and his stipend stopped from the Colonial Bishoprics Fund. The laity was kinder: at the same moment he was elected honorifically to the Athenaeum.

I think he was taken aback to discover quite what fools people are; and, 'speaking generally the *cowardice* of men in England is something amazing. The truth will prevail, I doubt not; but it is painful to me how little *love of truth* there is among those from whom one hoped most.' His old friend, the mixed-up F.D. Maurice, one of the original Apostles at Cambridge, now even refused to meet him. Truth about the Old Testament did ultimately prevail, but—people being what they are—it took a hell of a long time. Meanwhile, 'in one word, I am as strong, and cheerful, and full of hope as ever.' No Colenso was ever a coward.

On the subject of the Descent of Man Soapy Sam got his come-uppance from Huxley at the famous confrontation at the British Association meeting at Oxford. Disraeli put this palaver in the right perspective with his dismissive, 'Speaking for myself, I am on the side of the angels.' A no less vocal defender of Scriptural Inspiration was Dean Burgon: 'The Bible is none other than the *Voice of Him that sitteth upon the Throne*! Every book of it—every chapter of it—every verse of it—every word of it—every syllable of it—(where are we to stop?)—every *letter* of it—is the direct utterance of the Most High! The Bible is none other than the Word of God—not some part of it more, some part of it less, but all alike the utterance of Him who sitteth upon the Throne—absolute-faultless–unerring—supreme.'

1. We may append a footnote on him. At the time of the Indian Mutiny he preached a sermon calling for vengeance on the mutineers, when Queen Victoria was all in favour of mercy. Gladstone might have made this High Churchman archbishop of Canterbury; the Queen would never have had him. Tait, a real statesman was her personal choice. However, Sam got the fat bishopric of Winchester, where a fall—from his horse—did him in.

As some evidence of the kind of people Colenso had to contend with, we recall that Burgon, very influential at Oxford, regarded the disestablishment of the quite unrepresentative Irish (Protestant) Church as 'the nation's formal rejection of God'; was scandalised by Temple's being made a bishop, led a public protest against liberal Dean Stanley preaching before the university, and insisted upon its retention of the Athanasian creed, with all its nonsense. He opposed the abolition of religious tests for entrance to the university, and lodging-houses for students as giving ground for immorality. He regarded the reforming commissions as 'irreligious', and denounced the education of 'young women like young men' as 'inexpedient and immodest.' He was unmarried; in *The Lives of Twelve Good Men* he wrote a tremendous best-seller, for it appealed to an overwhelming characteristic of the age—humbug.

Bishop Lee of Manchester was in simple agreement with Dean Burgon: 'the very foundations of our faith, the very basis of our hopes, the very nearest and dearest of our consolations are taken from us when one line of that Sacred volume, on which we base everything, is declared to be unfaithful or untrustworthy.' Once again we see ordinary minds incapable of confronting the issue straight—*true or not true?* Colenso expressed himself surprised at *all* the bishops being ignorant of Biblical criticism. And they took no notice of his assurance that 'the object of my work is to show that the real value of the Bible, as a teacher of divine truth [we may omit that clause], is not affected by the unhistorical character of certain narratives, or by other errors in matters of fact which the progress of critical, historical and scientific research may detect from time to time in other parts of the Sacred Volume.' Today every bishop would accept the common sense of that, while commonsense itself omits the otiose 'sacred'.

Exposing the myths of a universal Flood covering the whole earth, and the Ark coming to rest upon Mount Ararat, appears easy game today, but a hundred years ago almost everybody accepted them as factual. Colenso went on to show the unhistorical character of Exodus, the utter impossibility of the numbers given in the Bible, exaggerated as Colenso well knew was the way in all early literatures. He took the trouble as a mathematician to compare the incredible numbers given with the extent of the land available in Canaan, let alone the impossibility of their subsistence in the desert conditions of Sinai. He went with care into measurements of tabernacle and Temple, let alone Ark, and showed the impossibility of containing the numbers given. Hence Holy Writ was not infallible. He did not directly attack the miracles of the sun and moon struck still, the waters of the river Jordan standing up in heaps, etc, but contented himself with pointing out that the tradition in which they occurred was itself unhistorical.

From the point of view of pure scholarship Colenso was able to establish the composite character of the Pentateuch, differing strata by different authors at different times—no question of a single Mosaic authorship, as people supposed, if indeed there were an historic Moses. This question he did not raise. (One sees what nonsense it can give rise to in Freud's crazy book, *Moses and Monotheism*.) As for the literal Inspiration of the Bible, *à la Burgon* and almost everybody, he explained that he had been forced to go into it from the necessity of his position as a missionary bishop. Already there were missionaries who would not put the Old Testament into the hands of the natives, the savage and bloodthirsty vengeful passages were so immoral in effect—the many places where the ancient Jews were commanded by their deity to exterminate their enemies.

At the conclusion of his First Part he described flatly 'the *groundlessness* of that notion of Scripture Inspiration which so many have long regarded as the very foundation of their faith and hope.' This was a blow which Protestants were bound to feel peculiarly, for at the Reformation they had taken their stand upon the Bible, and nothing but the Bible. Colenso was very much a Protestant and described 'the shock which I experienced at first, on perceiving the unhistorical character of the Mosaic narrative.' Catholicism was much wiser, or luckier, in not basing itself upon such a shaky foundation. This enabled Newman, for example, to be more open-minded about Biblical Criticism than his former brethren of the C. of E. Still, he had his own disingenuousness. When the Bible said that the sun moved round the earth, and modern science that the earth moved round the sun, never should we know which was

right until we know 'what motion is'! Colenso was able to reply
to both forms of cant that there was no infallible Book any
more than there was an infallible Church, or infallible Man.

He disclaimed any intention of applying himself to New
Testament criticism 'at present', though one sees a further
vista of trouble and condemnation for him if he had done so.
For it appears that Jesus, brought up as an orthodox Jew,
accepted that Moses was the author of the Pentateuch as his
fellows did. Colenso glimpsed the chasm that opened up, and
covered himself with the usual cloudy distinction between the
human and the divine. (The ancient Greeks and Romans had
not found it necessary to regard their deities as infallible.)

What was he to offer 'to supply the loss, something to fill up
the aching void, which will undoubtedly be felt at first, where
that faith which has been built only or mainly upon the basis of
the historical truth of the Pentateuch, must be in danger of
collapsing together with its support?' He cited the Apostle
Paul, whose Epistle to the Romans, he had translated anew
and 'Explained from a Missionary Point of View', as the
sub-title ran. Colenso supplied the answer, for the faithful.
'The main essence of that teaching is that our righteousness is
wholly of *faith*, a living trust in God's Love—that we *must* all,
and we *may* all, depend entirely on our Father's Mercy, and
come as children to His Footstool continually, for light and
life, for help and blessing, for counsel and guidance and, if
need be, for that "loving correction" which "shall make us
great".' Colenso was a good man, himself filled with that
sense. Whether it can be reconciled with the fact of universal
human suffering is another matter—certainly C.S. Lewis's
perverse *Problem of Pain* does nothing to answer it.

In Part II Colenso went forward to take the offensive. He
knew that many of the more intelligent clergy no longer
believed in the Flood or the Ark. He put an awkward facer to
them—he was an awkward customer. 'What are they to do
under these circumstances—those, I mean, who have their
eyes open to the real facts of the case, and who cannot bear to
utter what they know to be untrue in the face of God and the
Congregation?' He appealed to his fellows' sense of truth.
Actually he was supported by the laity in Natal, and his book
made such a sensation that people crowded to hear his

sermons in the cathedral—especially visitors, for he had become a celebrity to see, if not to understand. What they heard was not at all sensational in manner, just argument and analysis in the 'high and dry' Cambridge way; while Dean Green, an Oxford High Churchman, listened and totted up points for a trial for 'heresy'.

In England all Hell broke loose, if that is not too strong a term for bishops and deans sedately assembled in Convocation. The *Speaker's Commentary* was put forth quasi-officially to meet the demand to know what was what about the Old Testament: Colenso roundly condemned it for evading all the problems and points at issue. All the bishops, except Tait and Thirlwall, were ready to condemn him and expected him to resign his see. The statesman among them all, Tait, on his way to becoming archbishop of Canterbury, tried to damp down proceedings against the offender. Tait himself, however, had an Achilles' heel. He had been born a Presbyterian—had he been properly baptized and confirmed? Were then all the holy orders he had conferred *valid*? This opened up horrid, unsettling thoughts. His faith must certainly have been strong, for when Dean of Carlisle five of his young daughters died within a matter of weeks. In his letters one finds him and his wife going back pathetically to visit the little mounds of their graves.

Colenso had some more fun about the Ark, at the expense of a fool of a reviewer, who questioned, 'what difficulty can there be in accepting the hypothesis, which seems so likely, that these animals were further kept, during their sojourn in the Ark, *in a state of torpor*?' Colenso merely relieved himself with a couple of exclamation marks—such was the level of the replies directed at him. As our authority today, Professor Rogerson, notes, there were no answers, for no direct answers were possible. No use throwing the Early Church Fathers at him—none of them, except Jerome and possibly Origen, knew Hebrew.

One footnote is of interest to us, for it shows that Colenso knew what went on in the mission field in New Zealand. As against his own conviction of God's love, as the basis of missionary work, he noted the deleterious effect of Old Testament example on the Maoris. In 1862 a visitor had found a *runanga*, a native council, 'determined to govern by the Levitical Law. Thus cursing, adultery, and witchcraft were to

be punished by Stoning [the old Jewish form of death sentence, plenty of rocks handy in that landscape], and so on
throughout.' In answer to the questioning visitor, 'the simple
reply was that, "if God had commanded it, it must be right,
and if it was right *then*, it could not be wrong *now*." ' Human
reasoning, the human foolery!

Colenso went on appealing optimistically to men's sense of
truth. As epigraph to each of his volumes he quoted from a
review of *Essays and Reviews* in the *Quarterly Review*: 'Not to
exceed, and not to fall short of, facts—not to add, and not to
take away—to state the truth, the whole truth, and nothing but
the truth—are the grand, the vital maxims of Inductive
Science, of English Law and, let us add, of Christian Faith'—
and then proceeded to belittle the authors' attempt to get at
the truth. Colenso might have taken warning; he was certainly
taken aback by the storm his scholarly work provoked, he
expressed his 'amazement'. But a scholar with no illusions,
A.E. Housman, could have told him: 'The sense of truth is the
feeblest of men's emotions.' Even a plain historian knows,
what Lecky found: 'Men will believe anything without evidence, against the evidence, or in spite of the evidence, but
hardly ever in accordance with the evidence.'

Colenso was in England in 1862–3 to see his volumes through
the press, to face an immense outcry, inhibited from preaching
in various dioceses— only the modernist Dean Stanley welcomed him to his pulpit at Westminster. Bishop Wilberforce,
Soapy Sam, took the lead against him. What one notices in the
usual technique with such people—they never squarely confront the issue, they never answer the argument. Was Colenso
right, or was he wrong? (I have found the same obtuse obliquity
with regard to my work, inaugurating a new period in our
knowledge of Shakespeare.) Soapy Sam wrote that 'much harm
has been done among the young' by Colenso's book—not
whether it was true or not; 'it is doing an amount of evil which it
is difficult to estimate'; Colenso's arguments were but 'the
repetition of old and often-answered cavils.'

Could Wilberforce answer them? Colenso threw down a
direct challenge to the chief instigator of the persecution

1. Rogerson, 234.

against him. 'I would ask the Bishop of Oxford before my fellow countrymen—"Does he, a Fellow of the Royal and other Scientific Societies, believe unfeignedly in the literal historical truth of the account of the Creation, the Noachian Deluge, or the numbers of the Exodus?" No answer was forthcoming; the wily Wilberforce knew better than to reply. He was able to assure the House of Lords, however, that Colenso 'had always met from his seniors at home brotherly counsel—the kindest and tenderest counsel'—to deny this was 'a statement diametrically opposite to fact.' We see that that was a statement very much in character. Lord Houghton, the layman Monckton Milnes, rebutted this and deplored the 'unkind treatment' Colenso had received from his fellow bishops. From Natal he wrote to thank him: 'nor have I had a single line from any of the English or Irish bishops conveying an expression of sympathy, advice or remonstrance.' Since they could not answer him, they simply cut him off, outside the fold—or herd.

In fact our leading authority today tells us that 'nobody was able to produce what *today* looks like an effective answer to Colenso. Indeed the attempts at refutation look today like the last desperate defence of a paradigm that was soon to collapse. . . To Colenso more than to anyone else may be due the fact that in *scholarly* circles from the 1880's the defenders of the old orthodoxy were hardly to be seen, and the field was dominated by a new critical, if critically conservative, school of scholarship.' That was, however, after Colenso's death in 1883; while he was alive the poor man was treated with contumely and abuse, friendships broken, family ties dissevered, the family ostracised by its own; and of course in the popular media of the time caricatured as a monster, whose 'doubts' he owed to the Zulus. We now have seen enough to know that Colenso's were not 'doubts' but certainties, and they were unanswerable. This was what enraged people. Then, after his death, his epoch-making work was ignored, himself forgotten. That was the only way they could deal with him.

The Bishop hardly ever complained of the treatment he received—a deeply reserved man about his own personal, emotional life, he was a good deal of a stoic, even more a Christian gentleman. But his wife—whose own family cut her

off for her husband's misdeeds, as we learn from her highly
intelligent Letters (she was in intellectual agreement with
him, able to follow his work)—knew how much he suffered
inwardly, though he would say nothing.

That is why I am speaking up for him. I am not interested in
the minutiae of Old Testament scholarship, or theological
disputes about non-sense propositions, let alone the infantili-
ties of folk beliefs. The historian is interested in the insight
this gives into the character of men's minds, and the exposure
of the illusions with which they wrap up facts and evidence.
Why? Can't they face them?

For Colenso's many contributions to Biblical scholarship in
detail we must go to our authority. However, we must in duty
give some idea of the progress of his work, if only in outline.
Professor Rogerson tells us that as it progressed it gained in
sensitivity and confidence. There was development in Colenso's views of his findings; and, as we should expect from so
exceptionally honest a mind, if he changed his conclusion as to
some particular point, he was not afraid to say so. The fabric of
his achievement stands.

Though there was not a single scholar in the England of his
day qualified to accompany him, in the middle of his work he
was cheered to have won the respect, and agreement, of
Kuenen, the able Dutch scholar who was a leader of Biblical
Criticism on the Continent. Kuenen was himself influenced by
Colenso's findings, who was happily able to quote a long letter
from him in Part IV to say so. 'It was Colenso's *Pentateuch* Part I
which convinced Kuenen of the lateness of the narrative parts
of the Elohist source [one of the two main strata in *Genesis*].
Although Colenso did not judge his own work in this way,
Kuenen's shift in opinion was to have profound consequences
for Old Testament criticism.' So even though Colenso neither
was, nor is, acknowledged his work did thus enter into the
main stream of Biblical scholarship, if indirectly.

Kuenen is a name still cited today by Biblical scholars,
Colenso not. Nor was the latter's work much noticed in
Germany. That need not surprise us: German scholarship has
usually—from the 19th century on, at any rate—been sufficient unto itself, and German scholars not notable for recog-
nising the work of others.

So far from being shut up by all the hullabaloo and abuse, Colenso repeated his main findings—the composite character of the Pentateuch, no Mosaic authorship, different strata and dates. He now went on to demonstrate that *Deuteronomy* was later than the other books, and was compiled after the Exile to Babylon, or possibly during it. Right again. As for the Book of *Chronicles* it was quite unreliable historically. *Tobit* he treated as the fiction it is, and the stuff about the Tower of Babel quite properly as myth.

What I find most interesting is the increasingly anthropological character of Colenso's treatment of Holy Writ. Anthropology, as a discipline, was in its infancy then; but Colenso would have made a first-class anthropologist, as he was a first-class scholar. This was the more understandable from his position as a missionary, but an exceptionally observant and sympathetic one, on the frontiers of two cultures, and the almost unique understanding he had of the backward one.

It is amusing—and how it must have provoked conventional asses—to watch the hardihood with which he went on to treat their cherished fables in the light of the folk tales of other peoples in antiquity. 'We have thus seen that the statements in Genesis, chapter I [about the Creation], if regarded as statements of historical matter-of-fact, are directly at variance with some of the plainest facts of natural Science, as they are now brought home, by the extension of education, to every village in the land. It is idle for any minister of religion to attempt to disguise this palpable discordance.' It was for one thing 'a stumbling-block in the way of the young'—a nice way of retorting upon Soapy Sam *his* concern for the young.

Colenso went on to illustrate from other peoples' folk tales about the Creation of the world in antiquity. And not only in antiquity: he could parallel the observances of the ancient Hebrews, their feasts and fasts, from the Zulus in a comparable state of civilisation. This must have seemed irreverent in itself to the blind devotees of Holy Writ, as to less excusable Fundamentalists of today. 'The Zulu keeps his annual Feasts, and observes the New Moons, as the old Hebrews did, though he has not learned, in his natural state, to divide the month into weeks.' I do not know whether he goes into rites of circumcision, and the nasty habit among the natives, of female circumcision.

He devotes a chapter to Stories of Paradise and of the Fall of Man in other nations. (A pity that C.S. Lewis was not acquainted with this.) Colenso quotes at length from German authorities 'the Persian myth, describing the Fall of Man, which bears a striking resemblance to the story in *Genesis*.' So too with stories of the Flood. 'Many heathen nations have traditions concerning either a universal or a partial Deluge.' He quotes some of them, including the Chaldean, which came closest to the charming Biblical myth. Various peoples had attributed to an earlier period in their own history 'what, as we now know from the teachings of Geology, may have happened vast ages, perhaps even millions of years, before man lived upon the face of the earth.'

We see that he was well acquainted with the new geology, though here too conventional old-fashioned geologists would not accept the facts either. However in the course of these controversies—about geology, natural history, the antiquity and descent of man (Darwin, Wallace, Huxley, Lyell)— Colenso became a close friend of the foremost geologist Lyell, who was not afraid to face facts any more than Colenso was. For a prime example of the way religious belief could confuse and bring low a Victorian mind otherwise distinguished in scientific work, we might take the case of Edmund Gosse's father, an eminent zoologist and naturalist, a Fellow of the Royal Society, as described in the son's *Father and Son*. 'My father's attitude towards the theory of natural selection was critical in his career. Every instinct in his *intelligence* went out at first to greet the new light. It had hardly done so when a recollection of the opening chapter of *Genesis* checked it at the outset... Geology certainly *seemed* to be true, but the Bible, which was God's Word, *was* true. If the Bible said that all things in Heaven and earth were created in six days—created in six days they were, six literal days of 24 hours each.'

One sees how necessary Colenso's work was to clear the fog out of men's minds.

Still, not even liberals liked to face the facts directly and simply, especially the more muddle-headed among them. F.D. Maurice—of whom Carlyle said that he had never known anybody whose head was such a muddle—dropped Colenso like a hot brick when he got into trouble. And this in spite of the fact that, when Maurice was in trouble, Colenso had courageously dedicated his *Village Sermons* to him. Really, Colenso should not have confided such trust in humans—one of the few things for which I fault him. Then there was Charles Kingsley, whose thinking was mainly emotional, and had been in trouble himself for his Christian Socialism. He wrote in his rash way, 'I know no stronger proof of the truth of the book of Deuteronomy, and of the whole Pentateuch than its ending so differently from what we should have expected, or indeed wished.' What about that for a piece of thinking?—But indeed *thinking* was never Kingsley's strong point. As to the *Pentateuch*, he went on to ask the ludicrous question, 'If Moses did not write it, *who did?*'

Colenso confined himself to exclamation marks at the sheer silliness, and commenting, 'As well might Boyle have asked in the famous controversy, "If Phalaris did not write the letters of Phalaris, *who did?*" ' Bentley, greatest of Cambridge classical scholars, proved that the Letters of Phalaris were forgeries, to the exposure of the young Oxford scholar, Boyle. We might not be far wrong in regarding Colenso as the Bentley of 19th century Biblical scholarship, at least in the English-speaking world.

We learn that as late as 1880 critical treatment of the Old Testament had still made hardly any progress, for Colenso's work had been obstructed, wilfully misrepresented, then ignored. We note that sales of the first volumes of his great work, because of the popular rumpus they caused, were good, while sales of the later volumes fell off. We may sum up for ourselves the general achievement of his work, over and above its specialist contribution to Biblical scholarship. This was the highly significant one of presenting ancient Hebrew literature rationally and sensibly, like any other ancient literature, as it might be Greek or Latin—and not 'divinely communicated information', as Victorian cant would have it. As such, we can appreciate it much better for what it is, in all its variety: folk tale and myth, some of it reliable history, some antiquated law and ritual instruction; the moral objurgations and adjuration of the Prophets—some of it salutary; the poetry of the Psalms, the erotic poetry of the Song of Solomon, some naughty stories like that of Susanna and the Elders.

Rogerson sums up for us the character of Colenso's mind and work. 'Colenso possessed a remarkable trust in the universal love of God for all mankind, expressed supremely in Jesus Christ. This made him at one and the same time such a remarkable missionary and such a fearless critic. . . Colenso was far more than a mathematician dabbling with Biblical figures and dimensions. By unremitting labour in the midst of an incredibly demanding life as a missionary he mastered, as. . . no English scholar had before him the technicalities of Old Testament criticism. Many of his observations are now commonplace in Old Testament scholarship'—and the man who made them commonplace forgotten.

What then had Colenso to offer positively in place of the beliefs that rested on the infantilism of Bible Protestantism? Certainly not what he regarded as the grosser superstitions and even idolatry of Rome. We must remember that he was a good deal of a Puritan; he saw himself as fighting over again the battle of the Reformation for freeing thought from medieval shackles. He even disapproved of much of the hymnology of the new *Ancient and Modern*, particularly the translations of medieval hymns by the High Churchman, J.M. Neale, as idolatrous. Indeed, we can see his work in part as a reaction against the Catholicising tendencies of the Oxford Movement, the return of medieval ritual, practices and superstitions, the High Church trend that was in fact to capture the old established Church of England—the submergence of which the former deacon, J.A. Froude, contemporaneously deplored.

Colenso's answer to men's need for religion was to be found in his life and work, its positive expression in his detailed Commentary on St Paul's Epistle to the Romans—the original work on which such an enormous (and superfluous) fabric of argumentation and conflict came to rest through the ages. Characteristically Colenso reduced the tortuous scolasticism of that restless Jewish intellect to simplicity—the message of God's love for 'the whole human race', Christian and unChristian alike. This universalism was a further rock of offence to the orthodox, for it did away with the necessity of priestcraft and its functions, the exclusiveness of baptism and the sacraments, etc. It was virtually a gospel without dogma. Once again he condemned the nauseating dogma of eternal punishment. 'Once for all let it be stated distinctly, there is not a single passage in the whole of the New Testament which supports the dogma of modern theology, that our Lord died for our sins—in the sense of dying *instead* of us, or dying so as to *bear the punishment* or *penalty* of our sins.'

One may well think so undogmatic and universalist a religion far more appropriate to the conditions of today, when belief in dogmas and doctrines has crumbled all round. When Anglican bishops believe no longer in Virgin Birth or Resurrection, Incarnation or Atonement, let alone metaphysical constructs such as the Trinity. Or when a scholarly Roman monk can remark to me of Transubstantiation—for denying which so many humans have burned each other: 'Whatever that may mean.' When the dogma of the Assumption of the Virgin, her bodily ascent into heaven, was proclaimed by Rome, the archbishops of Canterbury and York protested against it as having no Scriptural warrant. The Jesuit theologians behind their piece of non-sense were able to reply that it rested upon the same basis as other doctrines accepted by the Church of England. The highly intelligent Pope Pius XII thereupon explained that the dogma of the Assumption of the Blessed Virgin into Heaven was not a terrestrial fact, but a celestial fact, i.e. not a fact at all.

One would hardly credit the nonsense I had to put up with from believers on the subject. One well-known French writer, a friend of Proust but a penitent of the famous Abbé Mugnet, argued to me that 'our Lord would never suffer his mother's body to suffer corruption in the earth.' What about that for a bit of 'thinking'? The plain fact is that few humans, whatever their rank or class, race or colour, can think, in the strict sense of the word—but they don't know it. In these democratic days it is unfair to withhold the information from them, and a duty to tell them.

This was what Colenso was up against. I doubt if he realised it, for though an able, clever man, he was straight forward and clear-thinking, not a subtle one—and much too confiding.

As a scholar again he well realised the limitations of Paul's mind, in his Commentary on Romans. Mr Guy, in his admirable study of Colenso, is chiefly impressed by the historical sense evident in this work. 'He begins the book by stating that one cannot understand St Paul's message adequately without a knowledge of the times in which he was writing, his personal circumstances, his audience's background, and the condition of the church in Rome at the time. In the Introduction Colenso provides this information and argues that "it is impossible that anyone should understand his language in this Epistle— even in the Greek, much less in the English translation—who has not realised to himself in some measure the state of things at Rome at the time when the Apostle wrote, who does not keep that state of things in his mind all along as he reads his words".[1]

A plain man would think that that limited the relevance and applicability of the work, at least in large measure. Mr Guy continues, 'Colenso was to urge his critics time and again to approach religious issues historically, to understand the concrete living situation in which the issue under consideration evolved, before passing judgment, and not blindly invoke dead dogmas.'

This message has fallen upon deaf ears today, as much as in Colenso's own time. For in Owen Chadwick's account of *The Victorian Church*—by a Regius Professor at Cambridge—we find him thus dismissed. 'Colenso was a writer of text-books on arithmetic... He had some Hebrew and German, but otherwise no equipment for tackling the critical problems of the Pentateuch. He went quickly, beginning his studies on the Pentateuch after he read *Essays and Reviews*. The works of a very few German divines, conservative and critical, were sent out to Natal. His *Pentateuch* was produced from these and his arithmetic. He had no sense of history, no idea how to criticise documents, no wide reading, and no profundity of mind.'[1] We now know enough about Colenso to realise that such a judgement is disgraceful: the author of it cannot have read Colenso's work.

It is to rectify such continuing misrepresentation, even defamation, that I have undertaken this book.

1. Jeff Guy, *The Heretic*, 73.
1. q. Rogerson, 234.

Chapter V
Life in Natal

For Colenso's scholarly work he was condemned by a majority vote of the bishops in Convocation—little as they were qualified to judge a work of such specialist scholarship. He himself put the crux of the matter in a private letter, quoting Coleridge's words that the question turned on *who is qualified to interpret.* He knew well within himself and from the external evidence that only himself possessed the qualifications. The one dissentient from the Resolution in Convocation was the intellectual Thirlwall, who protested that 'it assumes a paternal authority which rather suits an earlier period in the education of the world; and it presupposes a childlike docility and obedience which are now very rarely to be found.' Certainly not in Colenso—or any recognisably Cornish temperament, in which pugnacity is apt to be equalled by obstinacy.

Not that Thirlwall was prepossessed in Colenso's favour: he disapproved of his 'indiscretion, rashness, hastiness of publication and too great confidence of judgment.' Only an exceptionally honest man would have published these strictures upon himself. We may say in his defence, *Que faire*? Somebody had to tell the Emperor that he hadn't any clothes on—and it fell to a lower-class man to do it. An upper-class type would have been more discreet—or more disingenuous. What Thirlwall stood for was the principle to think freely on these matters within the Church.

Matthew Arnold, in a disingenuous essay, condemned Colenso. He declared that 'the highly instructed few, and not the scantily-instructed many, will ever be the organ to the human race of knowledge and truth. Knowledge and truth, in the full sense of the words, are not attainable by the great mass of the human race at all.' In fact, Colenso belonged to 'the highly instructed few', and Arnold must have known that he was quite right. Arnold meant that he should have kept his views to himself—hence the suggestion that he should have written in Latin! Arnold's squirming did not prevent him from being regarded as a subversive influence himself by Lambeth. Benjamin Jowett was to be more forthright and sincere: 'Colenso made an epoch in criticism by his straight-forwardness. No one now talks of Verbal Inspiration. He was attacked bitterly, but the recollection of the attacks has passed away; the effect of his writings, though they are no longer read, is permanent.'

But this just tribute came, alas, when Colenso was no longer alive to receive it.

In England during 1862–3 he was a notorious public figure, famous enough to be celebrated in verse—Browning's

> The candid incline to surmise of late
> That the Christian faith proves false, I find;
> For our *Essays-and-Reviews'* debate
> Begins to tell on the public mind,
> And Colenso's words have weight.

During his two years in England he was as active as ever, pushing several volumes of his *Pentateuch* through the press, the printers responding with a speed incredible to us in our slack Trade-Unionised age. He travelled about the country, preaching where he was permitted—he was inhibited from several dioceses—in Westminster Abbey under the wing of benevolent Dean Stanley, in Balliol College chapel under Jowett's.

He went across to Leiden for confabulations with the recognised Biblical scholar, Kuenen—himself unrecognised, though in fact the two men were in large agreement. Kuenen at least respected Colenso's scholarship and critical expertise, and came over to England to return the visit. This must have given Colenso much satisfaction and fortified him in his struggle for commonsense and intellectual honesty, amid the fog of Victorian and ecclesiastical humbug.

Actually he had a great deal of support in high intellectual society in which he moved. He did not neglect his old associations in Cornwall, though we know little about them. In the autumn of 1862 we find him down at Fowey, and the now famous man kept up relations with the friend of his youth,

John Merrifield at St Austell. The Colensos acclimatised a bit
of Cornishry in faraway Natal. Mrs Colenso writes of their
scalding milk from their cattle at Bishopstowe and making
Cornish cream. Naturally, though unfortunately for the historian, they were not in touch with the numerous Cornish
miners in the Transvaal. But we find Colenso keeping up his
Cornishry by reading Norris, the scholar who translated the
cycle of miracle plays from the old language, where the
folk-tales were comparable to those of the Bible.

His friends now urged his return to Natal to carry on the
fight, for in his absence Gray was presuming upon his shadowy
claim to be Metropolitan to stage a 'trial' of his former friend
for 'heresy'. The judgment was a foregone conclusion. Colenso
took no notice of it. Gray then proceeded to pass sentence of
Greater Excommunication upon his colleague, though perhaps without 'bell, book and candle'.

When Gray followed up these steps by declaring the see
vacant and appointing Dean Green as vicar-general of Colenso's diocese, pending the appointment of a bishop to super-
sede him, Colenso was forced to appeal to the law to maintain
his rights. The appeal ultimately came to the Judicial Com-
mittee of the Privy Council, which declared Gray's sentence of
no validity. This did not prevent him from consecrating, with
the aid of Bishop Twells, a bishop for Natal with the bogus see
of Maritzburg. Twells twice intervened in the cathedral, with
the support of Dean Green. Ultimately Colenso was forced to
appeal to the Supreme Court of Natal, which awarded him
control of his cathedral and its temporal assets.

He had the support of the laity in his struggle, especially of
his friends, the official Shepstones. People felt that he was
being unfairly treated by the ecclesiastical authorities, and
this gave him a spell of popularity. He got an enthusiastic
welcome on his return; better still, it coincided with a
downpour of rain, much needed after a long drought. Nothing
would persuade the natives that this was not due to the return
of their 'Sobantu'—Father of his People. Congregations at the
cathedral swelled to hear and see him; but it was an unedifying
spectacle that Bishop and Dean held rival services therein,
until the law decided in Colenso's favour. How the heathen
must have rejoiced!

All this consumed time, energy, money. He could not himself bear the mounting expenses of all the legal actions—and imagine the correspondence it involved, the distraction from his missionary work! We need not go into the legal complications, and there were many–in the Victorian manner of Jarndyce v. Jarndyce. The essential historic issue is this. Colenso represented the old Church of England in Natal. Gray envisaged an Anglican Church in and of South Africa; in this he had the support of the Church at home, not only of Lambeth and the bishops, but of the Society for the Propagation of the Gospel and the Society for the Promotion of Christian Knowledge. The former of these had provided the funds for Colenso's stipend and for the mission work of the diocese.

These were now withheld. Henceforth he had to depend on his own resources and the aid of friends. The mission work was severely restricted, the school, which had done good work for blacks and whites alike, could no longer be maintained—no money to pay teachers. No money to recruit clergy to support Colenso's diminishing hold: the S.P.G. sent clergy into the field to oppose him. Gray's clerical vision of an independent Anglican Church in South Africa, supported as it was by the Church at home, ultimately won the battle. Colenso's flock dwindled after his death to a small congregation, though it still has its faithful remnant.

Meanwhile it was necessary to raise the cash to fight the long legal campaign. A Colenso Fund was started, and it is fascinating to see who his supporters were—almost a roll-call of Victorian intellectuals. Among them were the leading scientists, Darwin, Huxley, Sir John Lubbock, Sir Charles Lyell, John Gray, Keeper of the British Museum. The eminent naturalist, Sir J.D. Hooker, a regular correspondent of William Colenso who sent him hundreds of plants and seeds for Kew, told Darwin, ludicrously, that he was subscribing anonymously, 'as my poor mother would take it so to heart.' Among historians were Grote, Lecky, John Morley and, unexpectedly, Professor Freeman. Writers included Dickens, Walter Pater and Arthur Symons, a good Cornishman. The great Rajah Brooke appears—an empire builder, if ever there was one: along with Leonard Courtney of Penzance, an inveterate anti-imperialist and pro-Boer later in the South African war. Fitz James Stephen occurs with the lawyers: James Martineau, leader of Unitarian opinion; several public-spirited Wedgwoods and Lyells; Henry Huth, the collector and bibliophile. From Oxford we have Max Müller and the civil lawyer, Dr Watson, of All Souls; Vernon Harcourt from Christ Church. It is a roll-call of intellectual laymen against the clerics, except for Jowett, Dean Stanley of Westminster, Dean Milman of St Paul's, Frederick Temple of Rugby (later archbishop), and the Rev. Sir George Cox—to become Colenso's biographer.

The Carlyles were friendly, and made the Colensos welcome at Cheyne Row, a meeting place for the high-minded. Tennyson, who was broad-minded about everything (except sex), greeted the Bishop warmly: 'though all the world should shriek out against you, I would receive you with open arms.' Browning considered that 'Colenso's words have much weight'; Matthew Arnold was merely supercilious, as usual.

In Natal the Bishop received what Mrs Colenso described as a 'brutal attack' from a clergyman, a former pupil whom he had helped (one has had that experience too). With 'many insulting insinuations' this young ass 'decides that the Bishop has not the proper knowledge or qualifications for a Biblical critic. "The tendency of the Bishop's teaching is to all uncleanness such as cannot be written of without raising a blush on the pure cheek of woman." ' He had sent this on to 'My dear Lord' – one must remember the lordliness of a Victorian bishop, Colenso was regularly 'my lord'—with the hope that 'he will not find in it one unkind word towards himself.' Really, the obtuseness of ordinary humans, and what Colenso had to put up with from them!

There now occurred an episode which, so far from leading to the gaiety of nations, gravely shocked the good Bishop. One of his prime opponents, Gray's right-hand man, Bishop Twells, was exposed for sodomy. I do not know whether, a High Churchman, he was a practising celibate, which might offer some explanation, if not excuse. A local paper, oddly enough called *The Friend*, reported: 'A criminal warrant has been issued by the Clerk of the Peace for the apprehension of the Bishop of the English Church here [Bloemfontein], on the oath of Louis Beek and others, with the commission of the unnatural crime termed pederasty [sic]. We can only add that our small community has been intensely horrified, all society has been stirred to its depths, and faith shaken in human nature and mankind generally.'

There was no doubt about the matter: Bishop Twells resigned, and ultimately escaped from South Africa disguised, appropriately enough, as a sailor. Poor Bishop Gray was visibly shaken: 'Alas, alas, how does Satan rage against our poor church.' Bishop Colenso was no less 'horrified'—here was something that did not come within the range of his understanding. One would have thought that he would have known about it from the savagery of *Leviticus* on the subject, if not from native experience: all 30,000 of Cetewayo's braves had to be celibate, like spartan warriors of old.

Colenso has only one reference to it in his correspondence. 'We have been horrified by Bishop Twells's affair during the last three weeks. Of course, you will hear all about it in England. He came through this colony in disguise, passing Pietermaritzburg in the night, and hid himself somewhere in Durban until he could get away; which he found very difficult to do, as the port people and sailors were generally very averse to taking him on board. At last he got away as "Ephraim Brown" on board the *Minalto* for London. There is, I fear, no room to doubt his being guilty of the capital offence. It is the most amazing occurrence, and I need not say sent a terrible shock through all parts of south Africa.' It certainly can hardly have helped work in the mission field, but I fear we must add innocence to other characteristics of the good Bishop's mind and heart. Christian gentleman that he was, he could not refrain from pointing out that it was only Bishop Twells's presence that made Gray's sentence of deprivation passed upon Colenso, as one of the three 'judges', that made it canonically, at least, valid. 'As there is no doubt he has been long practising this abomination', Colenso expected that it would give some compunction to the bishops at home who had supported the sentence of deprivation upon himself.

For ourselves we cannot help wondering what happened to this interesting character, Bishop Twells or 'Ephraim Brown', and what was the end of his story

In 1865 the Colensos were shocked and indignant at the proceedings of Governor Eyre in Jamaica, which raised a furore

in England and divided public opinion from top to bottom.
Eyre was a tough Yorkshireman, a fine explorer who had made
astonishing journeys into the unknown interior of Australia.
For seven years, 1846–53, he had been Lieut-Governor in New
Zealand to Sir George Grey, whom William Colenso knew. As
Governor of Jamaica Eyre was faced with seething discontent,
partly in consequence of the trouble stirred up by the Civil
War in the neighbouring United States. Something like a
rebellion was premeditated among the black population, who
were some twenty-five times the number of whites. Mutiny
broke out, twenty Europeans were killed, and atrocities com-
mitted upon whites in country districts.

Eyre was convinced that revolution was in prospect, such as
had led to the black republics of Haiti and San Domingo, with
their notorious records. He declared martial law and repressed
the rebellion with unnecessary severity, some 600 people being
killed. Liberal opinion in England was aroused—John Stuart
Mill, Huxley, Herbert Spencer, Tom Hughes of *Tom Brown's
Schooldays* to the fore—and Eyre was prosecuted. Thereupon
his defence was taken up by a rival body, Carlyle disgracing
himself with his tract on the 'Nigger' Question, with Kingsley
hot (as usual) in support.

The Colensos were shocked—it must be admitted that they
were very shockable; and, with their moral absolutism, consigned the Carlyles to perdition—out of the question ever to visit
Cheyne Row again as in former friendly days. Kingsley too
met with Mrs Colenso's condemnation: 'Mr Kingsley indeed
suggests that wholesale destruction of human life, and the
suffering it involves, are slight matters in the estimation of our
Creator, [it evidently did not occur to her that, in that respect,
Kingsley may have been right], which accounts for his support
of Governor Eyre perhaps.'

The Bishop was a moral perfectionist, keeping his eye open
for miscarriages of justice everywhere. We find him working
himself up into 'a state of great indignation at a sentence
passed the other day in New South Wales'—some poor fellow
had been sent to prison for two years for 'blasphemy', a few
coarse expressions about the Old Testament. One wouldn't
have thought—to judge from the literature of New South
Wales—that its state of moral perfection was such as to

warrant such a sentence. But this was much in Colenso's line.
Life must have been very exhausting for him.

It is remarkable how closely the family kept in touch with
events and currents of thought at home, when they were so far
away, communications rather irregular. Bishopstowe itself
became a communications centre, with an extensive correspondence, the whole family very highbrow and literary. So far
from Chadwick's unwarranted stricture on Colenso's lack of
'wide reading', the whole household was very bookish, littered
with books, papers, manuscripts. The daughters were now
taking to the pen too: Harriet, the eldest, becoming her
father's right-hand—the Zulus called her his 'Staff'—became
the author of several books and tracts, carrying on her father's
work; Frances, who wrote novels under a pseudonym, also
wrote polemical books on the historic events in which they
were all shortly to be involved.

Mrs Colenso herself was very much an intellectual. Her
published *Letters* give one a vivid portrait of life at Bishopstowe
and in Natal generally. It is amusing (and characteristic) that
the three daughters did not mix with colonial society, considered too frivolous with young ladies throwing themselves at
the heads of the officers serving out there. (Poor things, what
else?) Actually, Frances and the gallant Lt-Col. Durnford fell
in love with each other; but, since he had an estranged wife at
home in England, and both he and Frances were so high-
minded, it seemed their lips were sealed.

Now they were reading Froude's *History* of the Reformation
period in England. Naturally they felt that it corroborated
their struggle against obscurantism, as in a way it did.
(Though the Reformation had its own obscurantism, largely
Biblical: a pity that the sceptical humanists, Erasmus, Rabe-
lais or Montaigne could not have won—impossible, however:
too intelligent for humans.) 'I should like it to be printed on
cheap paper and disseminated everywhere', wrote the Bishop's propagandist wife. 'How plainly the persecuting Spirit
appears, the old Satan who never dies, burning then, calum-
niating now. The *Church Times* calls Cranmer a base traitor and
Latimer a brutal bully! How easy it is by distorting history to
bring a mighty mass of argument to bear on the wrong side.
Historians seem to be the most effective workmen on the side

of truth in these days.' Well, it is the vocation of historians to expound what is true, rather than that of theologians.

Then she was reading Froude's 'Plea for the Free Discussion of Theological Difficulties', but was 'surprised to find one who must know better, taking up and echoing the popular cry against my husband, as if he had merely raked up old objections which had been long met. To have these sideblows, or thrusts in the back, from those who have at least not more articles in their creed than ourselves is worse, I think, than the open vituperation of the professed orthodox. It seems to me that the article in question insinuates disbelief in everything, but carefully so as not to involve the author in the reproach of disbelieving anything.'

This was a shrewd point, for of course Froude had fewer articles of belief than the Colensos. As the editor of *Fraser's* he had to be careful what he said. Under the strain of moralism he got from Carlyle, Froude was naturally a sceptic and believed in no metaphysical or theological nonsense whatever. But he had burned his fingers badly when young, by writing too clearly what he thought, in *The Nemesis of Faith*, and been made to suffer bitterly for it. Henceforth there was an undoubted vein of disingenuousness in the way Froude expressed himself on these matters, and Mrs Colenso saw through it. All the same, she derived 'the greatest possible enjoyment' from his book, 'quarrelling with it half the time, which is pleasantly stimulating.' We see her as more open-minded, more intelligent than most Victorian women, with their religious prejudices.

In 1875 the Colensos had the opportunity to meet the great historian. He was on a mission on behalf of the Colonial Secretary, Lord Carnarvon, to explore the possibilities of Confederation as a solution to the problems of governing the variegated territories in South Africa and bringing some order into their haphazard and divagatory administration. Naturally, orderly-minded administrators like Shepstone, plagued by the problems of Natal, a poor colony with too large and proliferating a native population, was all in favour of it, and bringing independent and richer Zululand across the border into its orbit. Froude found that Cape Colony, largest of the territories with the biggest resources to date, was immutably opposed. But the pressure for some sort of confederation was an element in the striking events about to unfold, which were to bring backward South Africa into the forefront of world news.

The shocking treatment meted out by Shepstone to Langalibalele and his tribe in the mountains, on the borders of Natal and the Transvaal, stirred Colenso's wrath. He proceeded to make himself the champion of the wronged chieftain and to rouse public opinion in England in his defence. Like all distinguished visitors to South Africa, Froude paid his respects to Colenso and was entertained at Bishopstowe. Mrs Colenso reported home that 'Mr Froude distinctly said to Papa that Justice is the only basis on which we can even with safety deal with them. He has also given his verdict in the case of Langalibalele to the effect that the treatment of that chief and his tribe (9,000 people) had been so bad that the difficulty in England had been to believe it.'

Mrs Colenso was not taken in by Froude's smooth manner. 'How therefore he can back up Mr Shepstone, or allow Sir Garnet Wolseley to back him up, I cannot see. He called here once and said that he was going to stay in Natal some months, and indeed he promised to come and stay here sometime. But now he is gone with Sir Garnet Wolseley, and I don't know when or whether he will return. I confess, quite between ourselves, I have not much faith in him! You know his *Short Studies on Great Subjects.* Our copy is so scribbled over with my indignant remarks that I thought it as well to remove it from the drawing room when there was a chance of his coming here to stay. He professes great friendship and sympathy with my Husband in private. Time will perhaps show what his professions amount to.'

Her instinct was right. The cagey historian, understandably enough, had no intention of being indoctrinated by the Colensos' views on the native question, or coming forward in public in defence of the unfortunate chief, Langalibalele. As for her tell-tale marginalia on Froude's book, this is a well-known hazard when authors are about.

Chapter VI
Sobantu—Father of the People

What catapulted South Africa into the forefront of world news, produced tensions throughout it and forced its problems upon a reluctant Home government, was the discovery of the diamond fields of Kimberley, followed by that of the gold of the Transvaal. Colenso, with his intelligence and foresight, at once grasped what it portended. He wrote that it would 'revolutionise South Africa'.

Hitherto it had been a backwater. Britain's main concern was the coast line, the strategic route to India, shipping and commerce. There now ensued a rush to the diamond fields, then a Gold Rush like that to California in 1849. Thousands of miners poured in from all over the world, though mainly from Britain—Cornishmen to the fore for their skill at mining. This fact at once shook up the Transvaal, hitherto a casual society of Boer farmers, torpid and impecunious, with a minimal government, inefficient and corrupt, at Pretoria. This was challenged by a rapidly increasing body of foreigners—Uitlanders—who were eventually to demand voting rights and some representation in government: the ostensible excuse for the disastrous Anglo-Boer war at the turn of the century.

We cannot here go into all this, but must restrict ourselves to the story as it affected Colenso, and his part in it.

Until the 1870's he had taken no hand in politics. He seems to have accepted Shepstone's policy as Administrator of Native Affairs, with its reservation of some two million acres in Natal for the natives. This made Shepstone unpopular with the white colonists, who wanted more land and, even more, black labour. The Boers had no such problem: they had their basically Old Testament religion, which enjoined slavery and in some of its passages encouraged the extermination of the Gentiles.

Nothing of this in Natal. The British had ended slavery and the slave trade (while the United States continued both up to the Civil War). Nor must we fall for the simplicity of holding that all right was on the side of the blacks and impute all wrong to the whites. Underlying everything was population pressure, as we see everywhere in the 20th century—the gravest problem before the human race, as scientists well realise, and ordinary people, as usual, do not. Uncontrolled proliferation is the gravest danger before mankind, and the differential between black and white rates of reproduction is a continuing, if insufficiently appreciated, source, of tension, inevitably leading to conflict.

Natal was heavily overpopulated with blacks; polygamy doubled, trebled, quadrupled reproduction. With any sense of responsibility, one cannot but deplore any explosion of population. Zululand next door was underpopulated as the result of Chaka's ravages and massacres, sometimes driving whole tribes out of the country. Among these were the Hlubi who took refuge in the mountain fastnesses of northern Natal, while other broken remnants streamed in as refugees to add to Shepstone's worries. One cannot but have some sympathy with his later reflection: 'Had Cetewayo's 30,000 warriors been in time changed to labourers working for wages, Zululand would have been a prosperous peaceful country instead of what it now is, a source of perpetual danger to itself and its neighbours.' We must admit that there was something in that. Moreover, looking over the border, he saw that richer, yet more sparsely inhabited, country as a potential safety valve for Natal's surplus population.

Colenso perfectly understood the reasons for his friend's unpopularity. 'There are many here who *hate* the 'Shepstonian policy', because it treats the natives as having rights as men and Britsh subjects—who want to have them under their feet as "hewers of wood and drawers of water" for the white colonists, many of whom are ignorant and of low origin. Moreover, there are scheming politicians here who long to have *Responsible Government* [democracy!] because then—they know, or they *think* they know—the Government at home will leave them to manage the natives as they please. These worthies are *now doing their very utmost*, with the help of Sir Bartle Frere [recent newcomer as High Commissioner] to overthrow Mr Shepstone and bring in Responsible Government, and the consequent coercion of the Natives. "More taxes to be paid by them! More work to be done by them! Let the 'niggers' be under the white men's feet!"— such is the insane cry which is every now and then raised by our white colonists. And Mr Shepstone stands alone, keeping the howling mob at bay.'

This lets us into Colenso's mind, in his forthright way: we see that he had no illusions about the white colonists. Hitherto he had not interfered in politics, though in accomplishing his linguistic work to aid Zulus and whites alike 'he had the political rights of the natives very much in mind.' He expected to be castigated for this too. 'I have taken care to let the people know all about the Legislative Council, and their own right to vote for members, when properly qualified. And I hope to have a good many voters before long upon this Station.' This was as early as 1858, within five years of taking up his burden. It is clear that he envisaged a progressive vote for blacks as they qualified for it, as on the economic side he wished to see black peasant proprietorship as the objective for land settlement.

Overriding all this was his religious belief in a God as Father of all men, and therefore all men as brothers. His constant aim was to convince the blacks of the good intentions of the British government at home, to which he would appeal, with all the resources he had—though he was only one man to fight their battle—in any miscarriage of justice by the representatives of government on the spot. No wonder he didn't want the 'Responsible Government' of the white colonists—he knew too well what that would mean for the blacks. Further, with his ethical ideals, all government should be in accordance with Justice, and tempered by Mercy.

Such was Colenso's programme for South Africa—far-seeing, but not illusory. Events forced him now to take a line in political action; and such is the irony of events, that it precipitated a breach with his closest friend in the colony, Shepstone himself.

Colenso trusted the natives, and they came to put absolute trust in him, which they knew instinctively he would never betray. Hence, quite early on, he earned from them the title which he most cherished, and wished inscribed on his gravestone: Sobantu, Father of the People.

One of the immediate consequences of the discovery of diamond and gold fields was trouble on the frontier with the Transvaal. The Hlubi people there took to working in them, and their young

men preferred to be paid in guns—a currency which irresponsible elements were all too willing to gratify. One must remember
the appalling conditions in the early mining fields—no
government, life a free-for-all, fighting, drinking, murder; an
all-male society; dysentery, typhoid, enteric, silicosis. (As for
drinking, my father's youngest brother was killed there because
the engine driver in charge of the skip was drunk; the eldest
brother thereupon sought him out to kill him.[1])

Gun running was an occupation that appealed to *l'homme
moyen sensuel*. Naturally enough, with the immense dispropor-
tion between blacks and whites, Natal prohibited guns to
natives and ordered them to be handed in. Naturally enough,
the Hlubi people on their mountain frontier neglected to do so.
The consequences that ensued remind one of the Massacre of
Glencoe, which has reverberated through the history books
ever since: a remote, backward people, misunderstanding and
mistrust on both sides, failure of communications, an explosion, massacre.

Langalibalele, chief of the Hlubi tribe—let us call him Langa
for simplicity: the whites couldn't pronounce his name—
Sir Garnet Wolseley always called him 'Longbelly'. When the
tribe held back from handing over their guns, Shepstone
summoned Langa to his presence. The chief prevaricated,
delayed, then refused to come. This infuriated Shepstone. We
must not interpret this in terms of conceit. He was the
responsible official, and his hold over the native population,
with the immense disparity of numbers, depended largely on
prestige. 'Face'—always a dangerous element in primitive
politics, came into it—and behind that the threat of force.

Shepstone undoubtedly felt that security was threatened—
and fear is a prime motive making for war. A force was
dispatched to the frontier, ran into an ambush and some men
were killed. Thereupon the whites took an almighty
revenge—in the sickening way as in the Highlands of Scotland
in the 1690's. The Hlubi were hunted through their mountains, smoked out of caves, the tribe broken, their cattle
impounded, starved out. Refugees arrived on the Colensos
telling their tales—and straining the resources of the station,

1. For the story v. my *A Cornish Childhood*.

though they did all they could to help.

The family was appalled by the disaster; when the good Bishop realised the full tale of it, he at once ended his twenty year long friendship with Shepstone—to the grief of both men. Colenso cannot have realised the element of ruthlessness in Shepstone, who for his part cannot have reckoned on the moral ruthlessness of the Bishop. No doubt the Administrator thought that his friend should realise his difficulties; he considered he had nipped a rebellion in the bud. Colenso considered only the consequences of the savage repression.

We can read the situation through the eyes of Mrs Colenso. 'We have a good many women and children of Langa's tribe here on our land. . . The neighbouring tribe of Putili, though their only crime is having harboured some of Langa's cattle, have been involved in the same ruin. It is iniquitous. I do believe this was done without, or rather against Mr Shepstone's consent, but he does not say. What would I not give that he could be cleared of all blame in the affair! You cannot think what a trial it has been, and is, to the Bishop to lose faith in the justice and truth of his old friend. The Bishop had one friend in whom he believed—but now the colony is a blank. . .' Worse than that, the colony was wholly behind Shepstone's impetuous action, and moved over to active hostility to the Colensos, who henceforth were utterly isolated and alone in the community.

'John is again at issue with the world in which he lives! It is useless to say to him, would it not be wiser to let things take their course. You cannot bring the dead to life, nor restore the thousands of victims of official cowardice and cruelty to their homes. John *can not but* lift up his voice against injustice.' When Shepstone found that the Bishop was opposing his action, he declared that it was 'war to the knife between us.' Henceforth the Shepstones were arraigned, with everybody else in the Colony, against the Colensos. 'The split between these two has been an immense puzzle to the world around. I don't suppose they, or perhaps Mr S. himself, can understand a man's sacrificing his own private friendships and public supporters on account of a question of wide general interest, of justice or humanity. Whatever he has done, whether in criticisms of the Old Testament, or his protests against the action of the government here against this poor Chief, it has always been because, like Luther, *he could not do otherwise.*'

Shepstone chose to interpret the whole affair as rebellion and brought the Chief to trial for treason, without any counsel to defend him in the proceedings, largely unintelligible to him. The Bishop felt bound to intervene, interviewed Langa himself to hear his account of events, and by his public protest at least managed to get the old man a defendant at the bar. All this cost money, and effort, and worry. Colenso was kept busy with appeals to the Legislative Council, the supreme court, and of course correspondence far and wide. At once he had to bear the brunt of the unpopularity of the line he was taking. 'These are dark days for us. The support of the congregations here, which was so satisfactory and increasing only a short time ago, is beginning to be visibly affected by the extreme unpopularity of the course which John has taken.'

No money was now forthcoming to employ a curate to help the Bishop with services in the Cathedral. Hitherto, until his irrepressible conscience raised its head again, things had been improving. He had got rid of refractory Dean Green, though we learn that his own appointee was at this moment 'a fugitive from justice'. (What had he been up to?) Bishop Gray was dead, and Bishop Twells—who knows where? On the other hand, Gray's man, Bishop Macrorie of non-existent 'Maritzburg', joined the hue-and-cry of the populace against his fellow-bishop, whom he did not acknowledge as such. 'Dr Colenso's action is universally condemned as most mischievous. He continues to foster a sense of injury amongst the natives, and has actually, I believe, obtained leave for the convicted and self condemned Rebel chief to appeal from the sentence of banishment—whose mildness in itself has been interpreted by the natives generally as weakness—to the Executive Council, and Colenso himself is to plead his cause.' Macrorie records his infantile pleasure, in view of Colenso's unpopularity, at being saluted at last as 'my lord bishop'.

The fact was that Langa had originally been persuaded to plead guilty, his trial a farce. As for the natives' 'sense of injury', Mrs Colenso writes, 'many have seen their fathers, husbands and brothers killed before their eyes, their cattle driven away, their stores of grain pillaged or destroyed.' Eventually the Bishop journeyed to Cape Town to see Langa, after he was sentenced to transportation and imprisoned, to Robben Island, then on to England to try and get justice for him—there was none in the colony. On the good Bishop's return to Durban all the shopkeepers shut their shops for the day as a sign of their disgust.

Meanwhile he had been ill with overwork and anxiety. 'The real reason of my dear Husband's illness is the distress of mind he has suffered about this business of the *pretended rebellion* of the two tribes at the north of the Colony. He has felt acutely not only the sufferings of many poor innocent people, but the utter failure of truth and justice on the part of one whom he has thought so highly of for years that he has defended him continually from the factious opposition of the colonial press, and always held him up at home as the man to be Governor of Natal.'

Now, in the course of Colenso's researches, he discovered that there was a skeleton in the Shepstones' cupboard, which had been concealed from him all along. Not for nothing was he a trained researcher, and his discovery was germane to Langa's case. Some sixteen years before Shepstone's brother, John, had been conducting a 'peaceful' meeting; supposedly unarmed, with a tribe when he suddenly pulled a pistol at them, which he had concealed; and in the ensuing fracas some twenty-eight tribesmen were killed. Langa knew about this affair, and it partly accounted for his mistrust, and rude treatment, of the messengers John Shepstone's brother had sent to him to account for himself. John Shepstone lied about this affair, then threatened to sue the Bishop for defamation when his researches on Langa's behalf brought it to light. The fact could not be denied, however interpreted. Colenso, always a past master at scrutinising evidence, was now becoming as expert in the law. No wonder his latest (and best) biographer describes him—*per contra* to a Chadwick—as 'tremendously talented'.

We may fairly comment that, though Langa's trial was farcical, he would have been given none at all by the Boers. However, legal doubts clouded the whole proceedings, and Colenso took full advantage of these. 'Not only was the sentence of banishment unknown to native law, but it was in itself illegal.' The Lieutenant-Governor had no authority to impose a sentence of transportaton. 'What is astonishing in retrospect is that no voice was publicly raised in Natal against this trial except that of Bishop Colenso. It was his intervention which compelled the Lieutenant-Governor belatedly to grant counsel to the accused.' When this brief was declined, Colenso prepared Langa's defence himself 'with his usual thoroughness and care.'

Meanwhile, with his practised pen, he produced a pamphlet, *Langalibalele and the Amahlubi Tribe* (1874), so that his case should not go by default in England, whatever the white colonists thought. (They were only ordinary people; Colenso not.) When his documents arrived at the Colonial Office, the official in charge was duly impressed. His Appeal and the Executive Council's judgment were both 'very able and ingenious documents'; but it appeared that the Bishop managed to drive both Lieutenant-Governor and Council 'into a corner'.

This did not save Langa from sentence of banishment; whereupon the Bishop applied for a writ of *habeas corpus* on his behalf. When this was denied, he decided to journey to England, to put Langa's case before the Colonial Office and public opinion. Altogether, he was irrepressible—another annoying characteristic to opponents. Nor was he defeated all along the line. In the break-up of the Hlubi tribe the colonists managed to get through an order allotting its members as servants to private employers. The Boers would have simply enslaved them. Here was a difference between Boer and British rule; and Colenso managed to get the Secretary of State at home, Lord Carnarvon, to quash the deplorable order.

His advice to the tribe was sensible and moderate. 'He advised the men who came to him for guidance to work for some years for the government, and with their savings to purchase individual holdings of land. His aim was to assist them to become small peasant proprietors.' That was not Shepstone's idea. Meanwhile 'it was left to the Bishop, with his very slender financial resources, to support and educate some of the exiled Chief's children, whilst allowing a number of his people to squat on Bishopstowe lands.'

Mrs Colenso was in hopes that the Bishop would get a subscription going in aid of the 'poor devoured tribes'; but his health now was not what it had been, the strain was beginning to tell on him. 'We shall want money very much in consequence of our connection with them, if it were only for the continual hospitalities involved in their coming here to hear news, etc. But

besides, this school, which is begun by some six or eight boys
will increase, we expect, and then the clothing and the feeding
will not be done for nothing. . . Very few people know as much as
we do of the heart of the black man out here, how sensitive he is
to the colonial hatred and contempt, and how grateful to anyone
who treats him as a fellow creature.'

All the Colensos accepted the responsibilities that went with
this, and were rewarded with love. Harriet, the eldest daughter,
took special care of the Hlubi people, who regarded her as their
patron saint. As the Bishop's strength grew less, he came to
depend on her. In his last years he was fully engaged in his
defence of the Zulu king, Cetewayo—after the Anglo-Zulu war
imprisoned along with Langa on Robben Island. When the
Bishop journeyed to Cape Town on his way to recruit help in
England—there would be no calling on Carlyle in Cheyne Row
now—Harriet acccompanied him. At Bishopstowe Mrs Colenso
was expecting a visit from Trollope, the novelist, but she had no
hope that he would take any other than the government's point
of view.

Colenso could not obtain Langa's release for all his
efforts—he got his own release from his burdens first. After
thirteen years' imprisonment the old Chief was freed, and
came straight to Bishopstowe. The Bishop was dead and the
big house had burned, with all his books and papers—really he
had had no luck. Several of Langa's wives, children and
grandchildren 'have been living here ever since he was carried
away captive, Sobantu having allowed them to settle and build
their huts. It is really very pleasant to see the reverence and
affection with which he seems to be regarded after all these
years by his people. The chief feeling of Langa on coming here
and seeing us was of lamentation that Sobantu was here no
longer. When someone remarked that we were looking forward
to building our house on the hill again, "When the house is
finished," said the Chief, "you will find how empty it is".'

The revolutionary tide which Colenso had foreseen would
sweep South Africa reached its first crest in the last years of his
life. It did not sweep him away: one sees him left standing, a
solitary rock, amid the shifting sands, the dangerous currents
and eddies all round, in the midst of which he died. He could
not influence events now, let alone control them; the utmost he

could do was to mitigate some of the consequences, speak up for victims, defend and protect sufferers.

There are inevitabilities in history, movements which cannot be controlled, even individuals who might be under control who yet escape it. Governments at home certainly did not want war in South Africa—always a secondary area compared with India. But Home governments cannot always control their local officials on the frontiers of empire, and are liable to give more heed to their advice on the spot than to a stray missionary bishop, however irrepressible. The remarkable thing is that Colenso's voice should have been heard at all in the tumult. The Colonial secretary at home said of his representative—Sir Bartle Frere, High Commissioner, taking the bit between his teeth—that, without a telegraph line, he could not reach him on the spot, and he doubted whether, even with a telegraph, he could control him.

Sheer distance was an impersonal factor, as in the American Revolution—the Home government did not know what was happening, certainly not in time.

Here we must correct the contemporary misrepresentation of Colenso. Today we can see that he was in every way a man before his time. In his own time, in these affairs, he came to be regarded as an impractical humanitarian idealist. Of course that element was dominant in his make-up. But he was not an extremist, and he was no more impractical than the practical men of affairs who made such a mess of them, showed themselves as inefficient in action as in mind they were blinkered and stupid. In fact events showed them up as far more wrong than Colenso was. Nor was he unpatriotic. He was a patriot, both as regards his country at home, and the country he had come to identify himself with.

He stood for the good name of England. He always used his prime influence with the natives to urge them to trust the ultimate justice of the government at home. He then did his best to see that government and public opinion were properly informed, that the native case was put before them—there was *no-one* else to do so. He acted in what he considered to be the best interests of all: of the natives first, of England, whose interest was to avoid war, and of Natal itself, though the colonists didn't think so. Here there was a plain conflict of interests. Colenso tried to build a bridge. One sees him at various junctures advocating a moderate course, not a hopelessly unrealistic one. Again and again not only his warnings but his view of the situation proved right, both more statesmanlike and more far-sighted. We can complain only that he was ahead of his time.

Over the fatal annexation of the Transvaal, for example: Colenso was opposed to it, and was right. Shepstone had gone to England and urged this course upon the government as the solution for the troubles there. In and around the impecunious Boer government at Pretoria there was a certain amount of support for the British taking over an apparently hopeless state of affairs. Shepstone made sure of a number of supporters, and assured the English government that to take it over would be popular. Government accepted his view, and sent him back as Sir Theophilus Shepstone, Administrator of the Transvaal.

Colenso was appalled at this retrogressive step. It proved an even worse failure than he foresaw, with ill consequences in every direction. Shepstone had reckoned without the Boer farmers of the high Veld, who found an obstinate and determined leader in Paul Kruger—of whom the world was to hear much.[1] The Boers rose in rebellion and inflicted a humiliating defeat upon the British at Majuba (the Zulus said that the Boers were good marksmen, as they were). Thereupon Gladstone's incoming Liberal government handed back the Transvaal. Colenso was jubilant and, as usual, in hope of better things.

For Shepstone it was humiliation. Colenso considered that for twenty years he had been 'humbugged and deceived' in accepting Shepstone's view of things in Natal. Theophilus Shepstone's career as Administrator of native affairs in Natal may be regarded as a success, in the circumstances of the time. He was a fluent speaker in Zulu and other native dialects; he was one of the few people to understood the Zulu mentality; he maintained a special relationship with their king, Cetewayo, who regarded him as a friend.

In order to bribe the Transvaal Shepstone betrayed his friend. We have seen that there was a territory in dispute between Zulus and Boers, ominously named the Blood River

---

1. To his dying day old Kruger believed that the earth was flat. One appreciates something of the difficulties the British had in negotiating with such a type.

territory. It was held in Africa that the Boers were always out
for land (we might add that the British were out for labour). A
Boundary Commission had pronounced that the territory in
dispute was properly Zulu territory. Shepstone had gone back
on this, reversed himself, and awarded it to the Transvaal. All
to no avail, for the Boers were unappeasable, and the conclusion they drew from the British humiliation at Majuba was
that they could hold up any British advance. This led in turn
to the disastrous South African war—to the British the 'Boer
War'—at the threshold of this century, of which the consequences have been with us ever since.

Such was the background, but again we must restrict ourselves
to Colenso's own rôle. The Transvaal was out of his sphere. He
did not rejoice at Shepstone's humiliation, the way in which a
distinguished career had ended in utter failure; he regarded it as
the consequence of a wrong course of action from the first. The
more pressing, indeed the overwhelming, problem was that of
Zululand, which was on Colenso's doorstep, and with which he
was intimately involved. The dominant fact there was that
Cetewayo had inherited from his savage uncle, Chaka—a
Napoleonic, if barbaric, aggressor—a militant force of 30,000
braves. These young spearmen were not free to marry—i.e. were
not to be regarded as having achieved manhood—until they had
'washed their spears', in blood. They were a force to be reckoned
with. Naturally their white neighbours regarded them with
fear—and fear and mistrust are potent causes of war. Lurid tales
were spread of the barbarities of Zulu rule—no doubt exaggerated; of executions, throwing offenders into crocodile pools,
torture, death for witchcraft, etc.

Cetewayo was represented to western opinion as a bloody
tyrant. This was untrue. Of course, as a ruler he had—like all
rulers (like Abraham Lincoln, by no democratic methods)—to
keep order in the nursery. The king made his case that he had
to punish offenders, and pleaded that he kept punishments to
a minimum. Cetewayo was an improvement on the great
Chaka (one thinks of Ivan the Terrible—or a Stalin). Cetewayo
was not a fighting man. But this consideration leads to a
doubt: could he ultimately have controlled his 30,000 warriors
without allowing them a 'washing of the spears'?

Cetewayo would not have objected to their fighting the Boers, whom he regarded, with reason, as their enemies. But he was never in favour of fighting the British, whom he regarded as friends. Now he was betrayed by Shepstone, whom he had regarded as 'father' and 'friend'. Colenso himself was betrayed by the missionary whom Cetewayo had permitted him to place in charge of his mission within Zululand: one Robertson, who went over to the other side and reported every kind of horror as happening within the black kingdom. All this was useful propaganda—used by the white colonists to whip up feeling against Cetewayo. Colenso was not taken in by it—did he for his part lean too much to the other side? He did not regard Cetewayo's warriors as a 'standing army', he described them as 'an armed people'. He was not afraid; he had their complete trust, as he deserved. At the height of hostilities, after the disaster of Isandhlwana, he offered to go in person to try and mediate peace.

He too was deceived in his hopes of the change to a Liberal government in England. He had high hopes of Gladstone, after his return of the Transvaal to the Boers. However, after the unpopularity of swallowing that humiliation, Gladstone could hardly incur further trouble by quashing the new High Commissioner in South Africa, Sir Bartle Frere. Frere was a forward man, an annexationist, determined to make hay while the sun shone, i.e. push on with a forward policy before the Home government brought pressure to bear on him—and Gladstone had a multitude of problems on hand, nearer home, Ireland foremost. On the other hand the Lieutenant-Governor of Natal, Sir Henry Bulwer, was not in favour of a forward policy in Zululand. He did what he could to hold it up, but like Colenso—to whose position he was closer, though without his sympathies—he was pushed aside by the 'logic of events', the implacable dynamic of history.

An excuse for intervention in Zulu affairs had been provided at Cetewayo's accession. The succession to chieftainships was often a murderous affair—like the murders within the princely house of O'Neil in Elizabethan Ulster, or elsewhere under the Celtic rule of tanistry. Cetewayo had needed Shepstone's support for the succession to the throne on the death of his father, Mpande. Shepstone responded with a bogus 'coronation', which gave him the opportunity to impose certain conditions, and therewithal a convenient excuse to interfere.

And of course there were occasions of dispute, misunderstand-
ings, a genuine inability often on the part of the King and his
indunas (councillors) to comprehend the import of the communications they received.

They could neither read no write, and so were dependent on
intermediaries. One man understood the Zulu mentality even
better than Shepstone and Colenso. This was John Dunn, an
extraordinary character whose career was more appropriate to a
Rider Haggard novel than the sober pages of history. I wish I
knew whether he was Cornish by origin—he has a Cornish name,
indigenous in Mevagissey. He was born in Natal—was said to
have shot the last elephant in the neighbourhood of Durban. He
was trader, huntsman, adventurer, and he won the confidence of
Cetewayo. He seems to have given the King good advice, and to
have been an honest broker—in so far as such a man could be
honest—until he judged which way the wind was blowing. When
it blew hard against Cetewayo, with the arrival of Frere and an
armed force under Lord Chelmsford to back him up. Dunn went
over to the side that must eventually win, and betrayed the King.

It was an unconscionable betrayal—though such a man would
of course have no conscience—for Cetewayo had treated him
with the utmost generosity. He had granted him a considerable
territory along the Tugela river, the boundary with Natal, where
Dunn lived as the 'White Chief' of his Zulus and lived their life.
At his death his will mentioned some 28 wives and over 120
children (there may well have been more—O polygamy!) At the
end he hoped to rule all Zululand, take Cetewayo's place as king,
against whom he had turned.

Such a man was anathema to Colenso—I do not know whether
the Bishop ever spoke to him. Shepstone treated him with cool
civility, but dared not break with him for he was a power in the
land—power and wealth were what he was after. How one longs
to know the full story of this fascinating ruffian. To Colenso he
was simply a scoundrel, though that was again too *simpliste*. Dunn
was in his way a politician, and knew how to rule—natives
anyway. The Bishop of course had hopelessly gone to the good:
Dunn, in his view, gone to the bad—or, in our view, merely gone
native.

Sir Bartle Frere took action before he could be quelled from

London. Cetewayo was presented with an ultimatum which he could not possibly accept—and Frere knew it. The crucial point was the demand that the King disband his warriors. He certainly could not have done that, and remain king. One further consideration: he could not have got his 30,000 braves to disband before 'washing their spears' even if he had wished to, any more than Langa could have got the young men of his tribe to give up their guns. We must make a distinction between the King, who was not a fighting man, was friendly to the British and wished for peace, and his fighting men. It is remarkable that he managed to control them as well as he did.

A considerable barrage of propaganda was mounted in the outside world against the barbarism of Cetewayo's rule, and Frere made an attempt to square Colenso by basing the case for intervention on humanitarian grounds. In this case, Colenso wrote, 'England would have done her duty, as a mighty power, in enforcing changes in the government of Zululand which would be highly beneficial to the Zulu people—*if these were all that was contemplated...*' He was even ready to assent to it, 'as a sign that England was still ready to discharge her duty as a great Christian People.'

The Bishop tried hard to believe in Frere's good faith and the sincerity of his professions. What Frere really believed, however, was in the potential of the independent Zulu kingdom for aggression, that Cetewayo was taking Chaka for his model, and 'has repeatedly urged the government of Natal to consent to his "washing his young warriors' spears" in the blood of his neighbours', especially the Transvaal (temporarily British territory). Frere argued that Cetewayo had rejected demands for reform, and that 'the Zulu nation, as the most powerful in South Africa was to lead the native races in shaking off the domination of the white intruder and restoring uncontrolled native rule.'

This was not Colenso's view, nor was it his estimate of Cetewayo's character, with which he was better acquainted than Frere. When he realised that Frere was waiting only till his military preparations with Chelmsford were completed, the Bishop was affronted, felt once more humbugged and deceived. The year before Cetewayo's kingdom was invaded, 'I did very urgently advise him to trust to the uttermost in the

good faith of England, and now that I see what has come of his
so doing, I am deeply grieved and, as an Englishman, ashamed
that I ever gave him such advice—though it was the only
advice I could give him.'

The invasion of Zululand, with the undeclared aim of ending
its independence, was carried out with marked inefficiency by
Lord Chelmsford in command. A three-pronged advance was
undertaken—one in the north, the main brunt in the centre, a
third across the Tugela in the south. We cannot go into the
campaign here—merely remark that the terrain was extremely
difficult, the forces bogged down by the difficulties of transport,
slow ox waggons, camp equipment, guns, ammunition, etc. The
Zulus had no impedimenta, hence speed, immediate thrust,
then dispersal and away. And they had immense numbers: their
main *impi*, the active army, at least 20,000.

The British evidently expected a walk-over, and undertook
the campaign with equal complacency and inefficiency. And at
Isandhlwana (18 January 1879), the central column met with
unexpected disaster. Unprepared and without intelligence—
in both senses of the word—they were surprised by the vast
Zulu *impi*, perhaps all of 20,000 spearmen with their assegais.
The column had encamped on top of a hill, but neither
entrenched themselves nor threw up defences. It was a
cardinal rule of Boer warfare always to construct a *laager*, an
unbroken round of waggons end-to-end, from behind which
they could direct their fire-power and display the mark-
manship the British had to face later—and came to admire, as
we see from Kipling's verses.

Unaware that a vast horde was approaching, Lieut-Colonel
Durnford—close friend of the Colensos, as we have seen—the
senior officer at the encampment at Isandhlwana led a considerable contingent out of it to scout in the vicinity. He too was
unaware that the great horde was upon them: he put up a gallant
fight but was slaughtered with all his men, like so many cattle. It
was generally held that, if Durnford had remained in the camp,
his contingent might have just turned the scale and enabled it to
hold out. He was blamed at the time, but not by Chelmsford
against whose orders he had acted—with the best intentions.
After the war Frances Colenso, who had loved this gallant officer,
did her best to clear his reputation with her book on the Zulu war,

with the aid of his brother, who contributed the chapters on the military operations. She too was a gallant spirit, nearing her own end from tuberculosis; her book is an emotional effort, a piece of advocacy for Durnford—whose body was found weeks after the slaughter and mutilation, identified only by his gold watch.

What happened, as seen from the camp, is described by Morris in *The Washing of the Spears*: 'for a distance of almost two miles, stretching back to the spur and stretching far beyond [the British position], the heights were black with Zulus; then the mass cascaded over the rim and began to pour down. Their numbers seemed endless.' Fire-power kept the attackers at bay, until ammunition began to give out. In the heat of battle it was found that the crates could not be unscrewed, while the 'mounted men had no bayonets.' Numbers prevailed, and there was a hideous slaughter. 'Not a single man from the six Imperial infantry companies had tried to leave the camp, 581 of them had died with twenty-one of their officers. Altogether some 900 of the troops, blacks from Natal among them, perished that day; the slaughter among the Zulus, before they broke through, must have been even more grievous.'

The disaster reverberated throughout the Empire (and the humiliation of the British must have encouraged the Boers in the Transvaal to rise). Still, as one goes into quiet churches in the English countryside one comes upon memorials to gallant fellows who fell at Isandhlwana: 'the price of Empire', I register as I look and reflect upon them.

It was a signal victory for the Zulus, but their King did not rejoice. Their losses had been fearful, and Cetewayo mourned: 'An assegai has been thrust into the belly of the nation. There are not enough tears to mourn for the dead.' It does not sound like the voice of an aggressor. 'He had an army, he had been invaded, and the army was eager to come to grips with the invader; but he was still temporizing and seems to have hoped that a show of his force might somehow free him from the impossible terms of the Ultimatum.' Now 'the spears had been washed at last, and the men were satisfied.'

Cetewayo has been given credit for not taking advantage of the opportunity to invade Natal while the way was open. In fact, he had given orders to his army on no account to invade Natal. It looks as if here too Colenso's judgment of him was correct—

though at the same time I doubt if his *impi* was in a condition to carry the war into Natal; as Colenso said, it was not 'a standing army' with the capacity or resources for a prolonged campaign.

However, the Colony was in a panic at the news of Isandhlwana, refugees and wounded streaming back; many they knew were among the dead. At this moment of crisis the Bishop spoke out to the Colony in the most remarkable sermon that even he ever preached. I am surprised only that, for once, there was no protest; there must have been a sober mood of facing the facts, if not repentance. He traversed the course of events that led to the tragedy—people did not know what yet lay in store for them. 'Have we then been "doing justly" in the past? What colonial doubts that what has led directly to this Zulu war, and thus to the late great disaster, has been the annexation of the Transvaal; by which, as the Boers complain, we came by stealth "as a thief in the night", and deprived them of their rights. . . That act brought with it as its Nemesis the Zulu difficulty with respect to the territory disputed with the Boers. Have we "done justly" here?'

We might interpolate here that, if the British had been truly Machiavellian, they would have confirmed that territory to the Zulus and left them to fight it out with the Boers. That would have meant a very different 'washing of the spears'. But the British were not so clear-minded; as usual, they muddled along—and so into two wars.

The Boundary Commission had awarded the territory to the Zulus. 'Did we even then "do justly"? I must speak the truth this day before God, and honestly say that in my judgment we did not. . . A Resident might have been placed in Zululand, with the hearty consent of the King and People, who had asked more than once for such an officer to be appointed on the Border to keep the peace between them and the Boers. His presence would have had great effect in forwarding such changes in the Zulu system of government as we all desire, being known to be backed by the whole power of England'. The Zulus had had a traditional respect, and friendly feeling, for the English even in Chaka's time and ever since.

Now, 'wherein, in our invasion of Zululand, have we shown that we are men who "love mercy"? Have we not killed already, it is said, 5000 human beings, and plundered 10,000 head of cattle [by which the Zulus lived]? It is true that, in that

dreadful disaster, on account of which we are this day humb-
ling ourselves before God, we ourselves have lost very many
precious lives, and widows and orphans, parents, brothers,
sisters, friends are mourning bitterly. But are there no griefs—
no relatives that mourn their dead—in Zululand? What doth
the Lord require of thee, but to do justly and to love mercy, and
so walk humbly with thy God?'

Here we have Colenso's mind and heart. He ended by
addressing himself to the practical situation, and interpeting
Cetewayo's message: 'this war is all a dreadful mistake, a
horrible nightmare. Is it possible that I am fighting with my
English Father, with whom I have lived all along in unbroken
friendly intercourse? I have no wish whatever to do so. My
young men did wrong in crossing at Rorke's Drift [the Border
into Natal]. I ordered them not to cross, and when I struck, I
struck only in self-defence. As Englishmen, speak the word that
no more blood be shed; let the war be brought to an end; and
give me only such terms as I and my people can accept.'

Once more the Bishop offered to go into Zululand to
mediate, and see if he could bring about peace. The offer was of
course rejected; even his partisan biographer thinks that it
would have done no good. Events had by-passed him. An
Imperial power could not be so humiliated. There had to be
retribution, 'honour' saved, and personal reputations repaired,
not least Lord Chelmsford's. The war had to go on—until the
royal kraal at Ulundi was burned, and the King captured.

Colenso devoted his remaining years and strength to the
defence of the prisoner. He had no further influence on events
in Zululand, which was left in upheaval from top to bottom, the
people starving. He watched it all with grief and dismay,
working harder than ever to arrive at the true state of affairs,
putting his critical faculties to work comparing government
records, Blue Books, official reports, newspapers, with his own
direct sources of information from King and People. He had his
own printing press at Bishopstowe, their case should not go by
default. Before he died he had printed some 2000 pages giving
his record of and conclusions on events. One might say that it
was a campaign like that over the *Pentateuch* all over again.

'The more I read of the new Blue Books,' reported the
indefatigable researcher, 'the more am I sickened with the

evidence it gives of Sir B.F.'s determination from the first to
bring on this War and to crush Cetewayo, who appears to me
to have acted nobly throughout.' That may be as it may
be—what is clear is that the Zulu King could not have acted
otherwise: to him it was a war of national resistance, and he
did have the support of his people. This was contrary to what
the colonists believed and put out; but their Bishop declared
roundly, 'I do not care a straw for the opinion of the *colonists.*'

The War destroyed the whole basis of his position, what he
stood for—and stood up like a rock to defend—though it did not
destroy his own personal standing with the blacks: that emerged,
if possible even more clearly. 'The fact that the invasion had been
initiated and prosecuted by Britain negated the basic principles'
upon which both his claim and his appeal had rested.

However the aim of the war was achieved—the destruction
of the militant Zulu kingdom and whatever threat it had
constituted. It was partitioned into some dozen or thirteen
chieftainships, bringing forward a couple of chiefs from the
north who had been opposed to the dominance of the Usuthu
clan—Chaka and Cetewayo's people in the centre—who proceeded now to get some of their own back by persecuting those
loyal to the exiled King. John Dunn, who had gone back on his
long friendship with Cetewayo to whom he owed his status,
was further advanced, his territory much enlarged—he
appears to have aspired even to the kingship itself. The bulk of
the Zulus remained loyal to their King, though they did not
know for some time whether he survived or where.

At the conclusion of the war the British at least left the land
to its people—which the Boers would not have done. These
now took the opportunity of Britain's embroilment to fight for
their own independence in the Transvaal. This brought the
uncompromising Paul Kruger to leadership. Like everybody of
importance in South Africa, he came to visit Colenso at
Bishopstowe, who discovered 'the hopelessness of getting the
former rough diamond, as he was, to look at the native
question from our point of view.'

All that Colenso could do now was to concentrate on
defending Cetewayo, as formerly he had fought Langa's case
for him. It was a difficult and complicated job. Public opinion
in Natal and at home was inflamed by the disaster, and the

losses, at Isandhlwana. In the colony Colenso was now subjected to regular attacks in the press, where hitherto he had had at least respect. It was immensely difficult to establish the true facts in the barrage of official documents, representing the views of officials, and to co-ordinate them with such information as he could get from the Zulus themselves. There was the obstruction of distance alone: 'the actors were separated by thousands of miles in Zululand, Natal, Cape Town and London. . . But Colenso saw his task as that of making sense of the confused reports reaching him. For his situation at Bishopstowe was unique. Only he had access to information on political developments in England *and* non-official Zulu sources, the ability to analyse them critically, and the means to keep his allies informed about developments in the different centres. Only if this was done would it be possible to counteract the misinterpretation of events coming out of Natal and Zululand from official sources, upon which the British government based its policies.'

Once more Colenso's expertise as a researcher came in handy, and in the last couple of years remaining to him he worked, if possible, harder than ever. In his daughter Harriet he now had someone fully capable of sharing the burden.

Once more, with regard to policy in general and the shaping of events, he faced disappointment. He entertained high hopes of the change of government in Britain and the Liberals coming to power with Gladstone. True, the forward policy of Confederation was ended, Sir Bartle Frere and Chelmsford recalled. But the situation in Zululand was profoundly unsatisfactory and disturbed; complaints came out of the ill-treatment of Cetewayo's people by their opponents, now that their situation was reversed.

Colenso was convinced that only the return of the King, upon satisfactory conditions—i.e the suppression of militancy, no revival of the addicts to 'washing their spears'—could re-establish order. To this end he set himself to mitigate the conditions of Cetewayo's confinement at the Cape and advocate permission for him to journey to England to put his case. In these limited objectives Colenso had success.

In 1880 he and Harriet journeyed to Cape Town to see the two African leaders whose cause they were fighting. They had some five interviews with Cetewayo, whom the Bishop had not seen since his mission to Zululand in 1856. These conversations served to enlighten both sides as to the truth of facts in dispute, the shortcomings of Cetewayo's rule, which had served to justify its overthrow. The King had been surprised by the gentleness of Sir Bartle Frere's manner on meeting him: 'he sat and spoke with me just as you are doing. His voice was as kind as yours is.' The Bishop 'felt obliged, in the interests of truth, to dispel his pleasing illusion as to Sir Bartle Frere's friendliness.'

More than that, the Colensos were able to arrange means of communication for Cetewayo to keep in touch with his followers in Zululand and to advise him as to the course he should pursue. They urged upon him to appeal to the sense of justice in England itself, and to ask permission to make the journey in person. Cetewayo was terrified of the sea, which in all his life he had never seen until he was transported from Durban to the Cape. He was willing to trust the Bishop in this as in everything—'the journey is not so bad really.' For his part Colenso now set in motion his campaign for the King to be allowed to visit England. Meanwhile he had success too in mitigating the conditions of the two chiefs' confinement. Moved from Robben Island to the mainland, we hear of them agreeably hunting hares together out in the country.

Cetewayo's personality was his own best advocate. From his arrival at Cape Town he insisted on appearing in European clothes, and made a fine regal figure. People were astonished to find—so far from the barbarous savage of propaganda (true enough for the murderous Chaka)—a personage to respect in dignity and bearing, and with an endearing touch of childlike simplicity.

This gave him a marked personal success in England, where his personality appealed to the generous side of people—as it would not have done to Boers or Germans. In August 1882 he was summoned to an audience with Queen Victoria herself at Osborne, who was no less impressed. She wrote in her Journal: 'Cetewayo is a very fine man. He is tall, immensely broad and stout, with a good-humoured countenance and intelligent face.' Shepstone, after all, was there to interpret; and the Queen, always at ease in her own regal way, found exactly the right words for the occasion. She gave him a welcome and said that 'I recognised in him a great warrior, who had fought against us, but rejoiced we were now friends.' There followed friendly talk about his voyage, what he had seen, her family and daughters. Her son Leopold was ill; the King walked out on the Terrace by the window for the ailing Prince to see him. As the entourage drove away, 'Cetewayo caught sight of me and got up in the carriage, and remained standing till they were out of sight.'

We may regard this as Colenso's last success. It prepared the way for Cetewayo's restoration to Zululand—but on conditions which made it impossible for him to rule successfully and led to civil war, the ultimate destruction of the kingdom and his mysterious death.

The Natal press blamed the upshot on Colenso, of course. He lived long enough to answer back: 'this is a monstrous untruth. The "mischief and bloodshed" has been brought about by the *mode* of Restoration adopted by Sir H. Bulwer, with Sir T. Shepstone's entire approval, by which the gracious intentions of her Majesty and the English people have been frustrated, and the Restoration turned into a mockery.' Cetewayo was in fact restored to about one-half of his territory, central Zululand of his own Usuthu people, but with his powers to rule crippled, his land ravaged by his enemies during his exile, among them John Dunn who had possessed himself of most of the royal cattle by which Cetewayo's loyal following lived.

Once more he appealed to Colenso. 'I am at a loss to know where to put the Zulu people. I am at my wits' end. I see nothing of my cattle, which are in the hands of those who took them. I am destitute. We are eating nothing. My only hope is in you, that you will make an effort for us, that I may recover my cattle. You are alone my father in whom I trust to help me.'

Colenso could do no more. In a last letter to William Ngidi, his pupil of years before who had raised doubts of Biblical folklore—'the Intelligent Zulu' of newspaper caricatures: 'My heart is very full of grief, I cannot find words to express it, for this splendid old Zulu people.' And then, he well recognised the politics at the back of it all: 'I quite hope that now you know that the Zulus are set at loggerheads by the cunning of white men who want to eat up their land.'

Actually, by the peace made with them, the land had been left to its people; but in the partition of the country, into some thirteen largely unnatural provinces that often did not coincide with tribal units, lay the seeds of the civil war that ensued and the ruin of the kingdom.

Colenso saw this coming, but was spared the sight of its consummation. 'My body and soul are crying out for *rest*, before I go home.' It is the first time that one hears the note of giving up in all that life of unceasing effort and struggle. He was not yet seventy, and must have been endowed with a strong constitution. He suffered from occasional illnesses—lumbago at one time—but his wife says that he would never complain, or give any sign of his feelings as to the continual attacks upon him. It was remarked of him that he 'bore no resentment.' I find that strange, even a little unnatural: it might have done his opponents good to give them back some of what they gave him. (His cousin in New Zealand, no less involved in controversy, certainly did—answering them back seems to have done him no harm, and relieved his feelings.) With the Bishop, there was an iron reserve: I suspect that it went back to the straitened circumstances of his youth. I find it rather grim; but those who knew him well bore witness that there was warmth of heart within and even a certain charm in his relations with people, not only blacks. He exposed himself by his unbroken willingness to bear other people's troubles, and was in the end exhausted by it.

A sceptical intellect, realising what fools they are and what messes they make, would think it as well to leave them to bear the consequences themselves. But, as we have seen, Colenso was no sceptic; he was a believer, under obedience to follow the Master in whom he believed. What irony, what stupidity, that he should have been persecuted for want of belief!

In June 1883 he was still at work, reporting to his confidant of the Aborigines Protection Society in England the true state of affairs in Zululand, the facts as he gathered and analysed them. His daughter Harriet reported, 'he got weaker and weaker, but still took an eager interest in his work, dictating to me notes to be inserted in the printed sheets, and asking for the news from the daily papers, though he said he did not care to hear the leaders in the *Times* and *Mercury* full of abuse.' It was the only sign he gave; the family does not appear to have realised that he was dying. Before the end of that month he was dead, 20 June 1883.

His wife wrote bravely, 'I cannot regret that we were not more alive to the situation these last few days. It would (it might) have distressed him, and what did he want with death-bed scenes, who was worn out in God's service? Rest was his great need.' This was singularly un-Victorian of her, when one thinks of the fuss Victorians made about death, the emotional orgies they indulged in—notably Victoria herself over the Prince Consort.

Strangely enough, he was given a remarkable send-off by the Colony where he was thought to be so unpopular. People evidently recognised the quality of the man, if they could not understand it. It was obvious that he was an international figure whom they were losing, and never likely to see his like again. In the closed-down little city, shops shut and shuttered, streets thronged, his worn-out body was laid to rest in the cathedral that had witnessed such curious scenes: the Bishop locked out by the Dean; the Dean reading the sentence of excommunication promulgated by the Bishop of Cape Town; then, the sentence of no effect, the Dean sulking in his seat while the Bishop preached; the unforgettable sermon of the day of Humiliation after Isandhlwana, when he brought home to the Colony the consequences of their course of action.

He had not been able to hold up the action, merely mitigate some of its consequences—so much of the course history takes is inevitable. His daughter Frances wrote: 'circmstances only made him the special champion of the African races. Wherever it had pleased Providence to place him, there he would have fought the same good fight—there he would have laboured, and would have died—as truly as he now has died—for the truth against all falsehood, for justice against tyranny, for pity and mercy against cruelty and revenge.' This was no more than the truth; as someone else said, Colenso would have gone to the stake, like the Reformers of old—he regarded himself as their successor—for what he held to be the truth.

At home the Astronomer Royal, a fellow Cambridge mathematician, was of an intellectual calibre to pay tribute to both sides of Colenso's mind and achievement: 'the one man who could fearlessly publish the truth on the most important subjects—to whom intellectually I owe more than to any other person in my life—and the one man who could make an exertion in the cause of political justice which no other person would make.'

'Two or three weeks after our dear Lord left us', Mrs Colenso wrote home, 'there came a dreadful account from Zululand that Ulundi had been surprised in the night, the [Royal] kraal burnt, the King killed and his family slaughtered. We looked at each other and each thought; "This would have broken his heart. Thank God for taking him to Himself".'

These were the faithful women of the family who carried on his work: Harriet, who wrote a Memoir of her father and carried on the campaign on behalf of Cetewayo's unfortunate son and successor; Frances, who wrote up the account of the Zulu war, then *The Ruin of Zululand*, and helped Sir G.W. Cox with his authoritative *Life* of her father before her early death from tuberculosis, like the third sister, Agnes. These good works, books and campaign, could no more hold up the tide of history than their father could do.

It is fascinating to the historian to note that the sheer fighting quality of the Bishop came out in his grandson—in a way that would have dismayed his pacifist aunts—in Col. 'Jock' Colenso, who won a name for his gallantry as a commanding officer with the Gurkha Rifles—again on the frontier of civilisation—the North-West Frontier in India.

In Biblical criticism the Bishop won his battle, but only after his death: it was not until the 1890's that the subject caught up with him, then by-passed and ignored him, as we have seen, until today. In the Church in South Africa, in the event, he was defeated and Bishop Gray, after *his* death, won. With the support of the Anglican episcopate at home the Church in South Africa established its independence of the state, as a province of its own, with an archbishop of Cape Town as Metropolitan—but, could even Colenso have foreseen, with a black, Desmond Tutu, as archbishop?

Colenso's own flock, representing the Established Church of England, dwindled into something like a sect on its own—at least Protestant, as against the Anglo-Catholicism of the Church of South Africa. It was good to have his name remembered by his faithful remnant—many of them blacks—and his centenary celebrated in 1983.

He was, in every way, before his time. Perhaps his time will come.

Book II

William Colenso of New Zealand

Chapter I

The Printer

William Colenso's personality, career and circumstances offer many points in common, and some in contrast, with those of his more famous cousin, the Bishop of Natal. As Cornishmen they were both frontiersmen, whose careers fell on the frontiers of empire and civilisation, the one working for the Zulus, the other for the Maoris of New Zealand. Both had markedly strong personalities, forthright, combative, utterly honest and altruistic, public-spirited, religious in a very Protestant evangelical way, both missionaries; outspoken, tactless, completely irrepressible.

Though there is much in common with their work, and its inspiration, for the well-being and bettering of the natives in South Africa and New Zealand, there is a notable contrast in their circumstances. John William Colenso was a university man, always a gentleman, who married into good society—a family life of complete happiness; as a bishop, moving in the best society of his time, well known and recognised in governing circles; a leading intellectual in his age, and something of a world celebrity.

His cousin William remained a class below all that. He was not a university man, but largely self-educated as a printer; he was intelligent and not ill-read, with an acute, controversial mind, like his cousin's, even more dogmatic and forthright. We may take his life in rather lighter vein than the Bishop's life of struggle—though William's was not without its drama (one can hardly regard it as tragedy), in the break-up of his marriage and break-down of family life, leaving him solitary and querulous, yet more successful than before, in a quite different way. His career was broken sharply in two: the first half as printer and missionary, the second half in politics, local and provincial, and as public official. Through a long life he continued his botanical work, foremost of New Zealand naturalists, with an entirely new flora to bring to light; and he continued to study Maori language, folklore, custom, anthropology, leaving large and valuable collections here too, if he had not the Bishop's trained critical scholarship.

William's missionary career ended in a reverberating scandal, and for some three years he went under: a disrespected man, vulnerable to abuse, of which he got plenty, something of a pariah in his community. From this he emerged successfully, made money, and became more of a public figure as a politician—but more controversial, and controverted, than ever. Like his cousin, he was constantly misrepresented; and, like him exceedingly individualistic, he laid himself open to misrepresentation. Unlike the Bishop, the Deacon—he never acquired priest's orders–had few friends. Neither of them had a sense of humour or they wouldn't have got into so much trouble—or taken so much trouble either. They were earnest Victorians, incredibly hard-working, strenuous and energetic.

I doubt whether they had any contact with each other. We know that William was acquainted with the Bishop's scholarly work; but, more narrow and orthodox in his beliefs, he would hardly have approved of it in his earlier, clerical phase. On the other hand, the Bishop—a very square, family man—would have been scandalised by William's fathering a half-caste child by a Maori girl, followed by his suspension by *his* bishop, Selwyn, and his dismissal by the Church Missionary Society.

Both kept up their contacts with Cornwall, the Bishop managing to return there in 1862. During all his sixty years in New Zealand William kept up the hope of returning for a visit, but never managed it. He sent plants and seeds home—and Cornwall has acclimatised a range of antipodean flora, including even New Zealand tree-ferns. In the end, a man of property, William was able to leave a handsome legacy to his native Penzance. Still more, both his sons eventually settled there, the half-Maori son, Willie, to marry his cousin, Sarah Colenso. So William's branch carried on the connexion at home in Cornwall, where the Bishop's more publicised family were part of wider English life.

We see that William's career, with its downs and ups, proceeded along a lower level, with rather more amusement in it, than the impeccable life of the Bishop. One further difference is that, at the age of seventy, William wrote a

fragment of Autobiography to explain himself to his half-
Maori son, with its understandably defensive note. Nothing of
that in the Bishop's life—he was not much concerned with
himself but almost entirely with his 'causes'. In consequence
we can penetrate further into the more egoistic and fractured
life of the Deacon.

William was born at Penzance 7 November 1811, the son of
Samuel May Colenso and his wife Mary Veale Thomas, and
baptized in the chapel of St Mary's[1] on the headland by the
curate-in-charge, C.V. Le Grice, a friend of Coleridge. At the
age of fifteen he was apprenticed as printer, bookbinder, etc.,
for the usual term of seven years. During that time he
developed his hobby of botany, which ultimately gave him
name and fame, and became a youthful member of the Penzance Natural History and Antiquarian Society.

Desperately serious-minded, like his cousin, his mind was
chiefly given to religion. 'I was the eldest of a very large family
and was consequently very much used to, and pleased with,
the company of children; indeed, owing to numerous adverse
family circumstances, no small portion of my early days was
taken up with nursing. As I grew up I had been a constant
attendant on all divine services, on weekdays as well as on
Sundays. On Sundays I generally attended five services,
Church of England and W.M. [Wesleyan Methodist]. Then I
became a registered Church member of the W.M. Society. At
that time in particular the candle of the Lord shone upon my
head, and I rejoiced in its beauty.' H'm!

A good-looking youth, full of vigour, with long flowing dark
locks and glittering eyes, he seems to have had no interest in
sex and disapproved of the customary jollifications of the
town, such as the bonfires and dancing on Midsummer Eve. A
marked interest in anthropology—though he did not call it by
that name—developed later on in contact with, and closely
observing, Stone Age man in the shape of the Maoris.

In 1833 he left home for London, with letters of introduction
to ministers of the various churches he had attended. How-

1. In today's hideous society the church has been vandalised, the reredos
painted by the distinguished Newlyn painters of the 1920's burnt.

ever, his not sticking to one sect was 'looked upon with disfavour by some among them. (*Galatians* II. 6). My private rule was to read some portion of the Bible twice daily on my knees, and to engage in prayer three times a day—and from that good old rule I have never wilfully departed.'

Though he attended Wesley's church in Lincoln's Inn Fields, he met with more kindness from the Secretary of the Baptist Society. Through him and contributing small pieces of religious writing to *The Pilot*, he became acquainted with the Secretary of the Church Missionary Society. He earned little, but had few wants, could repay his debts home, spare something for charity, and 'was happy.' The Swan Inn was where most of the C.M.S. missionaries stayed, and he often visited their Institute at Islington, where he might have become an inmate; '*but my whole heart was set on going immediately abroad and to my work for the heathen.*' Thus he got engaged as missionary printer.

There followed a farewell visit home—by ship from Bristol to Hayle—and last visits with friends, including a religious brother of the well-known reactionary Tory, Sir Richard Vyvyan of lovely Trelowarren. Colenso continued to correspond with this cleric from New Zealand.

There being no direct ships for New Zealand in those days, he embarked, with printing press and type, in the barque *Prince Regent* for Sydney, the voyage to New South Wales taking five months. Sea-sickness did not deter him from holding services, in fine weather, and contributing to the ship's weekly newspaper. At Sydney he remained for some time waiting for a vessel, 'as none could be found willing to make a voyage to 'New Zealand.' The couple of Anglican ministers there were much overworked in the licentious free-for-all described in the Australian classic, *For the Term of his Natural Life*. Colenso helped out with nursing, visiting hospital and gaol, where he spent 'two days and nights with a poor young man condemned to die. Indeed I was obliged to go on to the scaffold with him, when three were hanged together. It took years to lessen the startling reminiscences of that day.'

'At last in December I left Sydney in a very small craft, a fore-and-aft schooner of 35 tons for the Bay of Islands, N.Z.—chartered purposely at a high figure (such was the risk) to bring me to N.Z. The captain was a landsman, only the mate could navigate the vessel, but was given to drink and sometimes gave up—'for days we were drifting (humanly speaking), the sport of the winds and waves', in want of water, what there was stinking. 'On Christmas Day we sighted a Hobart-town whaler; it being calm our Captain went on board and brought back some water, coconuts and a good piece of fresh pork.' Weather continued fine, the prevalent wind bore them towards New Zealand and down the east coast of North Island. 'On 30th December we were off the entrance to the Bay of Islands, in the outer bay, almost becalmed. A settler, who happened to be out in his whaleboat with a Maori crew, rowed up to us and kindly offered to convey me on shore. After a very long pull I landed at 10 p.m. at Paihia, the Mission station, thus ending an eventful passage of 21 days.'

It was an appropriate introduction to the amenities, the hardships and excitements, of life in the early unsettled days of the new colony.

What an astonishing little New World this intrepid Cornish-man had landed in! From first to last he was fascinated, and—like so many of his cousins in South Africa, a prolific writer—his journals, letters, pamphlets, articles sent to learned societies as well as newspapers, give us a vivid record of New Zealand from earliest colonial days to the end of the century. Living to 1899 he practically spanned the story and took perhaps a more representative part in it—from missionary to politician—than any other figure.

Since Captain Cook had made this remote Pacific country known to the civilised world it had become the resort of some very uncivilised white men—whalers, sealers, traders—and a fine old time they had of it. Their trading centre was the Bay of Islands in the North Island—the South Island does not enter into our story: North Island contained three-quarters of the Maori people. Even so, not more than a couple of hundred thousand were there to inhabit an island almost the size of England—largely mountainous, earthquaky, rather empty. Only the river valleys, coastal plains, and select areas, mainly around lakes in the interior, were capable of much cultivation. Hence warfare for land was endemic before ever white men appeared to add to its ferocity with musket and shot. Nor need we subscribe to the anti-colonial sentimentality usual today, for the previous Maori invasions (in the first millenium AD) had displaced the indigenous Melanesian population— probably eaten them, for such was their habit. New Zealand had no animals, except the extinct native dog (which the Maoris may have introduced).

Maoris regarded the gun as 'the great god [certainly the most effective one] of the white man.' When an early missionary took a Chief to England, the brave returned with 300 muskets. He 'then proceeded to terrorise his ancient enemies. Near modern Auckland he killed 1000 men; another 1000 at the Thames [East coast]; as many more of the Waikato tribes [West coast]; and perhaps twice as many died on an island in Lake Rotorua.'[1] This lake sported one of the natural wonders of the world in its pink and white frozen terraces before destroyed by an earthquake later in the century. 'In the 1820s and early 1830s these savage civil wars led to heavy casualties and cannibal feasts unprecedented in pre-European battles fought with stone-age weapons. It is estimated that about 40,000 people were slaughtered. It has taken until the present day for the Maori people to reach anything like their former numbers.'

It must be admitted that food supplies were very restricted—largely sweet potato, fish, birds, the pith[2] of ferns dried and baked into cakes; so the killing and eating of prisoners was a welcome addition to the food supply. This was accompanied by dutiful religious ceremonies to their war and tribal gods (one is reminded of those horrifying humans, the Aztecs of Mexico.) We read of the ceremonial eating by a chief of the eye of a missionary killed during the Maori wars. Maoris believed that the soul dwelt in the left eye.

Altogether one sees that such a society was in need of the efforts of missionaries, though these loosened the bonds and undermined the structure of a stone-age society, interesting to anthropologists, but hardly to be regretted—except by sentimentalists. In any case the colonisation of New Zealand was

1. Keith Sinclair, *A History of New Zealand*, 42.
2. It is usually described as 'fern-root', but actually was the pith of the plant, not the root.

one of the inevitabilities of history, like the colonisation of South Africa.

The land itself was of unsurpassed interest and beauty. It had been isolated before the appearance of mammals—hence no animals to eat (except the prehistoric dog, now extinct). No animals to fetch and carry, no horses or oxen—so all movement meant walking or canoeing, in which the Maoris were expert. By the same token three-quarters of the flora were unique—a subject of endless wonder to Colenso: along with religion a chief source of inspiration in his life there. When he took, after his downfall, to politics one may say of it as Clemenceau said on Paderewski, the great pianist, becoming President of Poland: 'Quelle chute!'

Along with the good things introduced by the whites there were, inevitably, the bad; drink, smoking, new diseases. Of course stone-age man had his diseases before the introduction of those of civilisation: from archaeological investigation it appears that the brown man had not lived beyond forty on average. The missionaries introduced medicines and cures for disease: perhaps this gave them protective *mana*—a quasi-sacred prestige which helped on their work, though at every stage they were hindered by primitive taboos.

Many and exotic were the birds for the Maoris to eat. They had already exterminated the large, flightless Moa—as East Anglians exterminated our bustard in the 17th century. Once Colenso found that he couldn't fancy a feast of parrots complete with heads sticking up reproachfully out of the dish. On another occasion he had to wait all day in hot sun for an interview with a chief, who might not descend from his roof till sunset, the fool, for some ritual observance of 'shame'—I do not know the explanation of this nonsense, being neither anthropologist nor apologist for humans.

Such was the society Colenso came up against, and was to do his best to improve, when he arrived in 1834: a mere margin of white settlers in and around the Bay of Islands, with a fluctuating riff-raff of sealers, whalers, seamen, predatory 'birders' raiding for slaves, etc. We may judge their mentality from their popular saying, 'A musket-ball for every New Zealander!'—the sentiment of the normal *homme moyen sensuel*. This was very different from William Colenso, not a normal type: 'Would that I had the nature of a polypi, I would not hesitate to cut my members to pieces, and say to each, "Go forth, in the name of the Lord".'

Not very humorous of him, but it witnessed good intentions; he was a good man, up against sin. Riff-raff and settlers together were only a tiny margin on the edge of Maori civilisation. Such was the state of affairs that it was absolutely necessary for the government at home to step in, to keep some order in the nursery. This it did, with the utmost reluctance to take over more obligations and responsibilities, in 1840. By the 'Treaty' of Waitangi the native chiefs accepted the sovereignty of Queen Victoria; in return they were guaranteed possession of their land; land purchases were to be controlled by government (under an able administrator, McLean, who—like Shepstone in Natal—would have preferred native reserves). Actually there was land enough for all; the Maoris made no use of much of it, and were willing to sell for gold. As the settlers encroached the Maoris divided into sellers and non-sellers: this sparked off the Maori wars of the 1860s, which were partly inter-tribal though essentially with the whites, with the usual accompaniments of massacres, and some reversion to cannibalism, which the missionaries had tried hard to suppress. As one old chief said, Christianity was 'not a religion for warriors.' Fortunately for Colenso, he was by then out of the mission field.

When he arrived at Paihia, chief station of the Church Missionary Society, there were three missionaries with their large families, of whom the senior was the Rev. Henry Williams. Colenso, very much the junior and in the inferior position of printer and general hack, found him 'a strict precisian, very imperious and distant, yet kind-hearted; eminently fitted for his post at that early time in this then savage land.' William had to doss down in the lean-to of the vestry to the little chapel, the common cemetery outside. He had to make do on £30 a year, with a single man's rations of flour, tea, sugar, soap, malt and lamp-oil, also pork and potatoes 'when to be had.' From the first settlers broke in the land, introduced animals and plants, especially wheat, sowed crops, cultivated gardens on which they employed the natives who could be got to work—to which they were *not* acclimatised.

William shortly got rooms in the mission house, where he did all his own cooking and housework. 'For years I never knew a day of rest: Sundays and weekdays, day and night, it was work, work, work! In addition to the constant work of the printing press, etc, there was the daily Maori school for men and boys; the whole of the preparing and dispensing of medicine, the issuing of rations of flour, rice, sugar etc for the sick all round-about. I had also to learn the Maori language, on which my heart was set, and soon had a share allotted me of conducting divine service, both at the Mission Station and at Kororareka (now Russell) on the opposite side of the Bay.'

Kororareka was the resort of 'the scum of the coast, whalers, adventurers, ticket-of-leave men', escaped or ex-convicts, and was described by the eminent naturalist, Joseph Dalton Hooker—whom Colenso was to meet and become friendly with—as consisting of 'one bad hotel, three cheating stores, many grog shops, and more houses of ill-fame.' To the missionaries it was just 'Hell'; to which the unredeemed replied by calling the mission station at Paihia, with its chapel bell calling out across the waters, 'Heaven'.

Once Colenso had a characteristically odd and risky experience there. He was trying to retrieve the body of a murdered sailor from the *pa*, or encampment, of a chief nearby. He had penetrated the camp in spite of threats and met with physical resistance from the chief himself—who perhaps felt defrauded of a meal. 'It was only his *mana* as a missionary that saved him from death at the hands of the enraged and rum-sodden chief.'

No Colenso was ever wanting in courage; but it was said later that, for all his kindness and care of the natives, he was rather overbearing with them (unlike his cousin, the Bishop); though both treated them like the children they were, brown or black.

His inner life was much occupied with 'agonising' prayer. He suffered from 'nervous stammering'—which he eventually conquered; and—a rather common sympton with heterosexuals—had no musical ear. These were serious impediments to his aim of becoming an ordained missionary, in holding services, preaching, and necessary hymn-singing. Henry Williams, his boss, became an archdeacon; William Williams a bishop; Colenso got no further than to become a deacon.

The Williams brothers, with and for whom he worked, were a remarkable pair. Henry, the elder, had a full and gallant career in the Navy from his early years, serving in many actions in the Napoleonic war. In the bombardment of Copenhagen under Nelson in 1807 he served both afloat and on shore with the land batteries. He was in the last engagement of the 1812 war with the United States, when the *Endymion* captured the U.S. *President.* In taking the latter with a prize crew to Bermuda he nearly perished in a hurricane. Retired from the Navy, he took orders to go out as missionary to New Zealand, where he had immense influence. Especially after stopping an inter-tribal war by the peace of Hokianga. He was mainly responsible, through his influence with the chiefs, for bringing about the foundation Treaty of Waitangi; and thereafter for extending the missions down the east coast to the Bay of Plenty, to the Hot Lakes district, the Waikato river in the west, and to Otaki in the south.

In 1826 he was joined by his younger brother, William, the scholar of the two. He was largely responsible for the Maori translation of Bible and Prayer Book, and compiled the best early Dictionary and Grammar of the language. Colenso did the donkey work for him for eight years; yet, when Bishop Williams came to write his account of *Christianity among the New Zealanders* and was a neighbour of Colenso at Napier, he never mentioned him. By this time the Deacon was regarded as not merely controversial but unrespectable. He, however, was more generous: when Williams' linguistic work was attacked Colenso came to his defence.

'Printing the New Testament took a long time owing to the editor, the Rev. W.W., residing at Waimate, then a long day's journey distant, a Maori messenger going to and fro with proof and copy only once a week. With 1st and 2nd proofs—and sometimes the state of the weather above, or the swollen and rapid rivers below—the printing of 5000 copies octavo took a long time and was wholly performed by myself, often hindered by my many other duties.' Shortage of paper occasioned delays, or the paper coming from Sydney proved inferior. Colenso himself designed the type suitable for printing Maori, and bound several copies of the finished book to present to missionaries. Then came the printing and translating of the

Prayer Book, 'another long and toilsome job. Besides those two large books there were lots of smaller ones, school books, Gospels etc—some containing 20–50 pages; of these alone the separate editions were many thousands.' All this made 'an epoch in the history of the New Zealand Mission.'

In itself this was a factor to revolutionise Maori society, which had had no script—all the more remarkable the achievement of the missionaries in reducing the language to script. It was noticeable how readily the people took to reading—an intelligent people in themselves—and their avidity for the tales and readings of the whites. Like all primitive peoples they had their own cosmogony: it had in it the separation of sea and sky, and even a Flood, just like the Book of *Genesis*. Bishop Colenso could have added this example to the others, if he had kept contact with his erring cousin.

At New Year 1838 Colenso made his first journey down the east coast, with William Williams, as far as Poverty Bay. 'We spent some time teaching and preaching everywhere among large numbers of natives.' It was on such journeys that 'he gained much of his extensive knowledge of the people, their ways of thought, folklore, traditions, and poetry, and eventually obtained an understanding of the race rarely attained by a European.'

Here he first heard of the astonishing, and extinct, *moa*. 'I heard from the natives of a certain monstrous animal—some said it was a bird and others a person. It somewhat resembled an immense domestic cock.' This piece of folk memory was accompanied by the usual nonsense lore, about its having the face of a man, living on air, etc. It had apparently been extinct for some considerable time, but later excavations of its bones reveal it to have been the largest of birds, one species standing 10 feet high.

We have from this journey a description of what a Maori *pa* looked like: a triple stockade, the posts consisting of straight, stripped tree-trunks, with 'large carved full-length human figures painted red on their tops.' The Maoris had a passion for the colour of blood, and dyed their matted hair red. (We recall that the ancient Britons dyed themselves blue.) The Maoris improved their looks with elaborate, patterned tattooing (one observes the habit recurring among whites, with lower-class simpletons today.)

There follows an enthusiastic tribute to the navigational skill of the Maoris in their canoes in those dangerous, uncharted waters with their reefs and heavy Pacific swell; and to 'the singer of canoe songs—which is done both to encourage the paddlers and to enable them to keep time.' As for the mission work, 'it is a gladdening sight to see and hear the natives at prayers—generally conducted by a baptized native Christian—whose tall commanding figure, book in hand, loosely wrapped in a blanket or flax mat after the manner of the ancient toga, forcibly reminds me of Raphael's cartoon of "Paul preaching at Athens." If anyone's heart wants animating towards Missions, he should witness this sight.'

'I brought back with me from the East coast several young Maori chiefs' sons to be taught and trained. These remained with me some considerable time, and were not only taught to read and write but were nearly all baptized before they returned to their people. Two of them in particular did some good work as pressmen.' He also brought back with him pencil sketches of the landscape, of Poverty Bay and elsewhere; like so many Victorians, like Queen Victoria herself, he had a talent for sketching, useful in the age before cameras.

On his return to Paihia he fell ill—there was an epidemic raging which carried off a good many Europeans as well as Maoris—it sounds like diphtheria. While Colenso was ill, a curious episode happened. 'One of the finest and stoutest of the Maoris, a young man of twenty', who was devoted to Colenso, lay up outside his doorstep and would not move: 'he had heard of my danger and he took it to heart.' The doctor said that there was nothing wrong with him, but in the night he died. It seemed to be an example of the 'wish-to-die' to which Maoris were prone. Today people take refuge in the word 'psychosomatic', which explains nothing. Perhaps anthropologists can tell us if this faculty is recognised among primitive peoples—it might prove useful among the so-called civilised.

After his recovery he went for a change to stay with William Williams at Waimate, and took the opportunity—after much

prayer for guidance—to write back to Paihia to propose
marriage to Miss Williams, evidently Henry's eldest daughter.
In his letter to the young lady he said plainly that 'God and his
work had my heart and would ever be uppermost with me.' Sex
does not seem to have entered into it. Williams had a good
excuse for rejecting Colenso's suit on the score of his health—
'though I could not help fancying that if I had followed my letter
up I should have been accepted.' The Williams family were
upper-class; evidently Colenso was thought not good enough—
after all he was not even in orders.

So, when the Bishop of Australia arrived on a visit, William
proposed himself for deacon's orders. He met this prelate on
board *H.M.S. Pelorus*, and accompanied him ashore in one of the
ship's boats. 'Owing to the rough tumbling surf we were obliged
to land at the north end of the long soft shingle beach. It was a
sore trial for the Bishop to walk to the other end where the
church was, he being lame.' It was intensely hot; Colenso had to
help him along. They were late and, when they arrived, he had to
unpack the Bishop's trunk and array him in all his finery in full
view of the congregation. What was still more uncongenial was
that the Bishop was a High Churchman, and was to be followed
by another, the famous Bishop Selwyn, to become Primate of
New Zealand, with whom Colenso's relations were almost as
strained as his cousin's with the Metropolitan of South Africa,
Gray of Cape Town.

In the autumn William took the first of his independent
journeys to the Cape at the northernmost tip of the island, 'the
famed and sacred Reinga, or entrance into the nether world of
the Maoris, where no European had ventured before—to the
little known natives of those parts, but mainly for my health,
which was suffering from close confinement and overwork.' He
went across the neck of the peninsula by Waimate and
Hokianga, thence up the west coast. It was a laborious march,
often along shingle, a strain to *pakeha* (white man's) feet, in all
weathers—in fact, the second recorded journey by a European
to this sacred spot. He made pencil sketches of the coastal
scenes, the Cape itself stretching its neck out like a lizard into
the ocean, whence the Maoris had come. It was also a
venturesome journey, for the spot was holy: the spirits of
departed Maoris departed hither to return to whence they came.

On the way he had an awkward experience. 'I noticed a delightful little pool of clear cold water in a rock basin in a sequestered spot in a thicket, and, being thirsty, I drank from it.' This was seen by some of the Maoris of the place, and there was a long public debate about his transgression, and what should be his punishment. 'The water of that pool had never been drunk before by any human being, as it was the head chief's mirror-water.' Charming, and even poetic—but silly all the same. Colenso had great difficulty, pleading his ignorance of the sanctity of the dell, and much was argued against 'my temerity and its desecration, while some of them waited to see the expected results (*Acts* XXVIII. 6).'

Oddly enough, he suffered no ill effects from drinking the holy water—evidently missionary men were exempt from the operation of *taboo*. On he went to the promontory, where grew a solitary sacred tree, the root bleached white by the feet of the spirits. He would have liked to reach down for a piece of root, but feared that an accident would be proof of his sacrilege, so he contented himself with a bit of the venerable rock.

Thus equipped, he made his way back painfully, with scorched feet, by the east coast to the Bay of Islands.

His instinct for collecting went along with his exceptional gift for observing. He already had a collection of Pacific sea-shells, exquisite as they are. He made friends with the early Australian naturalist, Alan Cunningham, who put him in the way of professionalising his interest in plants, trees, flowers from his youth. He began studying botany in earnest, collecting as he went, often having to stuff specimens inside his shirt or to take off his jacket to make a bag for them. He began to report his finds regularly to Sir William Hooker at Kew and send them generously off to contribute to the younger Hooker's splendid work on the Flora of New Zealand, where Colenso's contribution was as generously acknowledged. Not so the traveller Dieffenbach, whom Colenso helped with all the knowledge at his disposal—to which the selfish German (so like them) helped himself in his book without any acknowledgment.

Often enough in Colenso's explorations of new unvisited territory he came upon evidences of the inveterate tribal wars which the missionaries were doing their best to bring to an end. Moving along the coast, partly by canoe, partly on foot along the beaches, he spent a night at Tohora, 'a deserted village the inhabitants of which had been massacred in some tribal battle, their bones now lying bleaching on the sand.' He climbed to the top of the former stronghold; 'as far as the eye could see there was no sign of human habitation. The whole countryside was depopulated or deserted.' (So—room for white settlers to move in and make the desert blossom like the rose!) He was rewarded by finding 'a curious little orchid now in bloom completely ornamenting the wilderness.' Then—a botanical discovery, to which his name was eventually given, the silver pine, *dacrydium colensoi*. He had heard of it from older Maoris—we see that he was in familiar daily contact and fluent in their language; this botanical rarity had not been noticed for some years, for it grew singly in dense forest. He managed to run it down, secure a branch and send specimens to Hooker.

He kept pets for companionship—a favourite blue penguin, for which he made a skin jacket with long cord to let it down from his garden for a swim in the bay. However, one day it bit through the cord and made off. He was usually accompanied by his dog. In all his travels he never saw a native dog: 'the last surviving native dog of which he could learn was killed as an offering to a *tohunga* [priest] on the occasion of the tatooing of a chieftainess in 1831.'

He noted the red oxide in the sea cliffs, from which the Maoris obtained their favourite colouring to decorate their buildings. The red pigment with which they decorated themselves was obtained by soaking fern fronds in chalybeate water with layers of ferruginous mud, then baked and made into balls—their cosmetics. Colenso found it a hard test of gallantry when a half-naked, haggard old lady with tangled locks, 'poured the contents of her rouge-pot over her head and face' preparatory to rubbing noses with the white man. He wrote an article 'On the Colour sense of the Maoris', and sent contributions reporting his finds and observations to various learned periodicals such as the *Tasmanian Journal of Science*. The tale of his writings, and printings of them, was beginning to mount up:[1] he had a full share of the family itch for writing.

1. cf. Bagnall and Petersen, 458–60.

Where his cousin the Bishop took *In Memoriam* with him on his journeys, William took Longfellow, his favourite poet— appropriately: Red Indians and all that. He noted the enormous fishing nets of the Maoris, when piled on shore looking like hayricks. Prize specimens of *moa* bones he sent to the eccentric Professor Buckland at Oxford. Witchcraft was as prevalent, and as dangerous, as among the Zulus. At one village he encountered a gathering of lesser chiefs around a sick head-chief, who was being soused with warm water in a wooden trough. His sickness was the result of being bewitched by a neighbouring tribe (well-a-day—one needed something to fill up the vacant hours, the Maoris not being given to work). Colenso knew the fatal consequences that might ensue from such childish convictions, and spent a long time trying to persuade the nursery that there was nothing in them—he did not know with what result. Oddly enough, Maoris were often intelligent enough to be persuadable, even by reasoning.

He could not but deplore their casual irresponsibility about their forest fires, depleting the natural wealth and beauty, laying waste miles of lovely woodland. At one spot only a few clumps of *kauri* were left, 'the remnants of a once mighty forest which had been consumed by fire. Some of these few survivors were even now burning fiercely, having been carelessly set alight by passing natives.' Even from this desolated area 'two new plants were collected, *coprosma crassifolia* and a small fern, *gymnogramme leptophylla*.' (I am reminded of Edward Lear's *manypeoplia upsidedownia*—philistine as this may seem to elect botanists.)

Colenso had the proper attitude towards trees, almost a religious sense of their independent life, their majesty and beauty. Again and again in his Journals he is overcome by the natural beauty of the strange land he was to make his home—and to celebrate. Near the famous Rotorua Lakes, of the natural terraces, he came upon a grove of *manuka*, 'which flourished here, growing in clumps and rows as if artificially planted. These trees were literally laden with a profusion of handsome blossom.' Or it was elsewhere, on the beeches a fine *loranthus* grew in thick bushes, 'bearing crimson flowers in profusion; so that, in some more open spots among the closely-growing trees the whole forest wore a reddish glare, especially on a western slope heightened by the beams of the setting sun.' One has the feeling that, accompanied as he was by native bearers, the spectacle of 'things growing' delighted his heart more and gave him as much companionship.

He was present at the prolonged discussions out of which came the Treaty of Waitangi, and wrote up an account of the proceedings to forward to the Church Missionary Society that employed him. The new government commissioned him to print off 200 copies of the Treaty; the incoming first Governor Hobson gave him encouragement in his good work. Later, when troubles accumulated, Colenso claimed that he had foreseen that the Maoris had not understood fully the implications of the treaty. The government was intended to control land purchase, but this did not always work effectively. Settlers jostled for individual sales, which some chiefs were only too willing to make. We cannot here go into the complications; but in general Colenso advised the Maoris faithfully in their best interest, usually not to make them.

Next year, 1841, was of decisive importance to him scientifically: 'for three reasons—the founding of a journal in Tasmania in which he could publish material.' During the next few years he published four scientific papers, and maintained a regular correspondence with its editor. Then came his meeting with the son of the great Sir William Hooker, the no less distinguished Joseph Dalton Hooker. At the end of the year he undertook his longest journey, into the unexplored mountainous interior. The wife of the celebrated Sir John Franklin, Governor of Tasmania, sent him a botanical microscope for use on his expeditions.

Altogether one cannot but be impressed by the energy, the ability and imagination with which eminent Victorians were pushing forward the frontiers of civilisation, enlarging scientific knowledge in their age, on a greater scale than ever before and in every field.

Joseph Dalton Hooker (1817–1911) had studied moral philosophy at Glasgow, and understandably thought that it 'had been of little service' to him. Far more valuable were his numerous voyages around those frontiers, to the Falkland Islands, Tasmania, New Zealand. He agreed with Darwin over the process of Evolution by natural selection—both of them had found support in the views of Lyell on geology and the antiquity of man (as against erratic Professor Buckland). Hooker accumulated astonishing collections, thousands of plants. In 1854 he published his magnificent *New Zealand Flora*, and in 1867 his *Handbook* to the subject to which Colenso contributed so notably.

Hooker describes for us Colenso's establishment at Paihia: 'a square *brick* one-storied cottage with a high roof in which was the printer's establishment as well as the owner's dwelling. . . They all seemed very busy, and the sheet of native language well struck off and ready to be dried. . . In the sitting room was a portrait of poor Alan Cunningham and a pretty pine tree in a bottle, as also some of my father's botanical works on a table. Mr Colenso talked of some fine collections he had sent home. . . Of shells Mr Colenso has 150 species, with many insects and minerals.'

As for the man, 'Colenso has been extremely kind to me. He is a very good fellow in every respect, his time however is too much occupied at present with the printing, and other higher duties of a missionary's life. Of this class of men Mr Colenso is among the most superior. He is now gone on duty to the Interior . . . he gave me some curiosities of this Island, including some *minerals* and a beautiful *papa nautilus*.' Hooker and Colenso made many botanical excursions together. Up the Waikare Inlet, 'the rich vegetation along the banks began to be enlivened by the *pomaderris kumeraho* coming into flower.' Hooker noticed the burnt forests on the hills, 'caused by the natives firing indiscriminately any part of the ground where they wished to commence planting and letting the fires run into the noble forests, where immense tracts of land are laid bare and timber of immense value wantonly destroyed.'

In the small space of one glen alone Hooker collected nearly forty species of fern, with other plants. Before the expedition left for the Antarctic Colenso was back to say adieu to Hooker. 'I am sure a warmer-hearted, happier-minded parson never came in my way. We formed an intimacy which shall never be forgotten by me. . .' Colenso sent a present of some porter and claret to the ship, 'though I am sure his poor cellar could ill afford such a diminution. . . He had sailed for the East Cape—many nice things he had previously given me, *minerals*, *shells, native ornaments,* etc. He intends devoting himself entirely to plants during this trip.'

A valuable testimonial from such a source. Such were the amenities of early antipodean life.

Chapter II

Marriage and Ordination

After seven years of donkey work as printer Colenso felt in
need of a change. He proposed it in an important letter to the
C.M.S. in 1840 making the proposal. He wished to make a
return visit home to visit his parents and family, as he had
promised he would do at the end of seven years. He wanted to
be ordained, and to find a wife among his own people in the
West Country. The C.M.S. found him too useful to grant him
leave. The Roman Catholics had started a mission now in the
Bay of Islands area—when there was plenty of room for them
elsewhere—and the rapid extension of the Anglican missions
necessitated more work from his press. As for a wife, the
missionaries had large families with disposable daughters and
did not see why he couldn't be as well suited from among
them.

Candid as ever—as all Colensos were—his Autobiography
lets us into his mind on the matter. 'I did not feel that pressing
want of a wife that many do, partly owing to my having been so
long and so thoroughly domesticated and drilled in by sheer
necessity to learn many household duties—cooking, cleaning,
sewing, mending etc.' But circumstances were changing, with
more and more settlers coming in, the interruptions of visitors
calling on him: 'the very Maori domestics were becoming
unsettled and often capriciously left without warning.' The
missionaries were not backward in advising him to look out for
a wife among their daughters. Sex does not seem to have
entered into the matter, or even to have raised its ugly head.

Having finished the big job of printing the Prayer Book at
last, he took a holiday to re-visit the East Coast. A little ship
took him south down to Hicks' Bay on the large eastward-
jutting peninsula; thence he proceeded south, walking along
the coastline and over the beaches south to Poverty Bay, to
stay a few days with the Rev. William Williams now resident
missionary there. He returned overland on foot, an immense

journey by the East Coast lakes, then across country to the West Coast to the mouth of the Waikato river; thence over the narrowing neck of the long northern peninsula back to the Bay of Islands. 'A most romantic and interesting journey, on foot—as indeed all my journeys were—accompanied with no small amount of peril and hardship.'

On his return he received a letter 'recommending to my notice Mr Fairburn's eldest daughter as a suitable wife.' He had seen her only once before when she was a small girl attending school for the missionaries' daughters at Paihia. She was now of an age to marry; he wrote to propose in an open letter to her father, and 'my offer was immediately accepted by both.'

Shortly after the scene was transformed by the arrival of a bishop for New Zealand. His ship, with his entourage, anchored in the Thames, with the Fairburns' mission station nearby. There the Bishop had a pre-view of Elizabeth Fairburn conducting the Mission Girls' School—the first he had ever seen—and formed a good opinion of her competence: she was fluent in Maori. Thence the Bishop sailed on to the Bay, landing at Paihia, where Colenso received him. It seems to have been dislike at first sight; or, if they were not exactly disgruntled at first meeting, they were not particularly gruntled.

Bishop Selwyn (1809–78) would have known the Colenso name, for he too had been a Fellow of St John's at Cambridge. Where Bishop Colenso had been a brilliant mathematician, with a First, Wrangler and Prizeman, etc, Selwyn rated a modest Second in Classics. But, tall and athletic, immensely energetic, he was a born leader. He had the advantage of belonging to the governing class—a great-uncle had been an associate of General Oglethorpe, founder of Georgia. He was at a preparatory school with Newman, then went on to Eton to win honours as an athlete. Appointed Bishop in 1841, he learned Maori on the long voyage out, and enough seamanship to stand him in good stead sailing the uncharted waters of the Pacific. Incessantly travelling, in six years he visited all the settlements in New Zealand, by this time both islands, and from 1847 began regularly visiting the Pacific Islands included in his immense diocese. Eventually he consecrated two bishops for North Island and two for South.

In his forty years of endless work he organised the Church throughout the new country. He had a fine record in regard to the Maoris, consistently opposing land-grabbing by the settlers and refusing to allow missionaries to acquire land for themselves. When the land question led to war in the 1860's undaunted he ministered impartially and indefatigably to both sides, and was misunderstood by both. That did not deter him: he was a great Christian gentleman. He was also an autocrat—and that was right in the circumstances of founder and organiser of the Church of New Zealand.

By the same token he was not an easy man to come up against, and he held all the power, certainly spiritual authority. Of course William Colenso came up against him— that might have been foreseen, given their temperaments. William was not one for submitting to authority; and, if he wanted ordination, he had to obey. He had only a small scope for independence: he was employed by the C.M.S., he was not one of the episcopal entourage the Bishop brought out with him. They were university men, whom he preferred for the priesthood, and he was insistent on the requirement of Latin and Greek. William knew Latin—I do not know how on earth he found time to acquire it (except that, a Cornishman, he was keen always on learning)—but I do not think he had any Greek. Then, too, Selwyn was a High Churchman. It was a little like Bishop Gray of Cape Town over again—except that William was more orthodox Evangelical than his heterodox cousin, not yet Bishop of Natal. A new epoch was to begin in church life in New Zealand, and in William Colenso's as well.

First encounter with the remarkable man who was to win, and deserve, fame as Primate of New Zealand—and after whom a Cambridge college was to be named—did not go well. William had written 'out of hours', and printed 'at his own expense,' a Tract against the Errors of Rome, animating on the conversion of three Roman priests who had been received as Anglicans by the Bishop of London at St Paul's. He had also written two tracts in Maori on the subject and had them printed in Sydney and Hobart-town.

At a gathering of all the neighbouring missionaries to welcome their Bishop, one of them came across to dress William down. 'The Roman Catholic priests don't like your new Tract at all; they say that the Conversion [at St Paul's] is all lies, and have been demanding authority for it.' The Bishop was paying great attention to this, when he weighed in with his judgment against all such writings. This was statesmanlike of him, and for good measure he 'came down heavily upon me as a *layman*' expressing opinions on such a matter—as if one could prevent any Colenso from expressing opinions!

Soon after this Selwyn went off on his first visitation of his enormous diocese. 'On his return he made some harsh remarks to me about the press, etc—all which I had considered to be wholly independent of him and outside his jurisdiction.' However, he was willing to meet William's desire for ordination; as soon as he had got things in order at Waimate, which he was making his centre, 'having such a very large suite who had come out with him.' William was to reside with him there for some four or six months to prepare for ordination.

A new printer arrived from England to take over the printing office; work now was much diminished, the essential heavy work on Bible and Prayer Book etc having been accomplished by William during his eight years' servitude. Other printing presses had now been set up, particularly at Auckland. Early in 1843 he got leave to go up the coast to visit the fair Miss Fairburn, and 'the conclusion we arrived at was that our marriage should be postponed to take place after my Ordination, say in about a year.'

This was not at all in accordance with the Bishop's wishes, who wrote 'almost ordering me to return at once and be married.' Then both were to join his establishment, where he needed Miss Fairburn to teach in his new Maori Girls' Boarding School at Waimate. 'I greatly disliked the Bishop's letter both in tenor and in tone, but at this juncture I could do little but obey. The Bishop, having got all the Missions, both clerical and lay, one by one in a most curious way, completely to submit to him in matters secular as well as clerical, was completely master of the situation.' Selwyn was, rightly, a masterful man. This was what it was to be one of the governing class.

The marriage seems to have been ill-omened from the start, neither partner having any affection for the other. William journeyed down to Auckland, near which the Fairburns lived, and arranged for a parson to walk over, across the scoria, to marry them. The night before the wedding was one of the worst he ever spent—not a wink of sleep. The prospective father-in-law was given to drink, got drunk and kept William awake in his bedroom next door with the disturbance he made and his mutterings against the prospective bridegroom. 'The house, a very large wooden one, was wholly unfinished within; the rooms were not yet all partitioned off, so that I could not help hearing too much—it nearly drove me mad. I packed up my few things in my valise: I opened the little window of my bedroom, a lean-to; I determined to leave them and go and hide among the fern and scoria until morning.' That would have meant leaving the Mission for ever: in the morning William thought better of it—though, writing forty years after, he was still not sure, the marriage led to such unhappiness.

Later he heard of cases where the bridegroom, one of them a minister, refused to take the hurdle 'at the very Communion Table rails'—William would not say 'altar'. 'Perhaps I ought to have done so—but I dare not decide.' If he had, we should have missed a good story, or all would have turned out very differently.

He remarked on two omens at the time. Walking into Auckland he was admiring a particularly fine hawk, when it alighted on the ground, and allowed itself to be taken. He took it back to the house with him—captive. The minister arrived late, having walked out through the scoria, and the pair were hurriedly married, with only a portion of the service read. William went down to the men's house afterwards to see how they were enjoying their little marriage feast—and found them crying bitterly apart, refusing to eat. Was this another example of the intuitive faculties of primitive people— etiolated by civilisation, like the sense of smell with so many highly developed persons?

Fairburn was already a man of property, and handed over land on the Tamaki as his daughter's marriage portion and to support her children, 'if any'. He offered William too some land, which he declined—like Selwyn, he was opposed to missionaries annexing land—though he had been given a small section by a settler friend at the Bay.

Thus began marriage under no auspicious circumstances, and William did not enjoy life under the cynosure of the Bishop while waiting for ordination. His wife was the only mistress at the school, to which a large number of Maori girls had been brought in from the *pas* around, who 'had to suit to harsh unsuitable rules.' The Bishop was, again rightly, a stickler for discipline. Elizabeth's work was heavy, day and night, 'to please the Bishop and his large party, among them several newly arrived English ladies with their own unsuitable notions.' William was called in too to teach them all Maori, and translate for the Bishop's own press—both Selwyn and his chaplain attended the classes.

'Many were the words, not a few were the scenes, between us'; William began to doubt whether he would achieve ordination after all. 'My thoughts and opinions were *not* theirs'; the whole atmosphere was rather High Church, uncongenial to a Protestant Colenso. When three of Selwyn's young men were ordained, William was left on the shelf. Elizabeth was wanted more and more at school, and worked to the limit of her strength. At length 'the Bishop gave me a travelling commission again to visit the East Coast Maoris, and return by a zig-zag course, crossing and re-crossing the Island from sea to sea, that he might know more fully the numbers and the villages of the Maoris.'

This was his third visit to the East Cape, 'landing, or upset and swimming ashore', thence on to Poverty Bay and south to Castlepoint.' He then struck across the peninsula to Hicks' Bay, and during the next months crossed and re-crossed the Island two or three times. No-one could have got to know it better: 'it was a long and arduous journey, shipwreck and heavy trials in an unknown country, where no European had been before me, and sometimes where neither Maoris nor Maori food were.' I suspect that his *mana* as a missionary and his fleuncy in Maori, still more his stamina, got him through.

He got back to Waimate in February 1844, some three weeks after his daughter Fanny had been born, to find his wife still very unwell. Thenceforward they occupied separate rooms and beds.

Before his ordination 'I was subjected to fresh and unthought-of trials from the Bishop.' There were the XXXIX Articles to swallow—which, contemporaneously in England, occasioned the young historians, Froude and Leslie Stephen, to reject their deacons' orders. Then there was the crucial doctrine of Baptismal Regeneration, over which there was much fuss in England. The Rev. Mr Gorham's rejection of it, and the sensible lay Judgment in his favour, triggered—if that was the word for it—Manning off into the Roman Church, to become a Cardinal. (He would never have been made archbishop anyway if he had remained an Anglican—too High Church for Queen Victoria.)

William was carpeted by the Bishop all the evening before ordination, some five hours of it, on these and other prickly subjects. 'The main thing in dispute between us was that I was always to obey him as to residence—even if against the direction of the C.M.S. [whose inflexion was distinctly Low Church]. I had long known that this was the particular point that the C.M.S. would not concede to the Bishop, and so I would not, could not, agree to do as he wished.' At this Selwyn told him plainly that he would not ordain him if he did not consent. 'My old and best missionary friend, Archdeacon William Williams, said that I ought to give way, and on his word I did so.' Next morning, on his way to church, one of the Bishop's chaplains called him into the house, and presented him with an episcopal order to sign, to the effect that he would keep no more than five head of cattle at a time. 'Remonstrance was of no avail.'

Formalities completed, the 'infectious hand of a bishop'–in someone's words—laid on his head, William found that he had been destined for Hawke's Bay by Selwyn, 'who said that the Church had no other suitable person to send to this new unknown and wild place.'

The Bishop laid down his instructions in rather lordly fashion. 'I have to request you to proceed to Turanga in the *Columbine* and place yourself under the directions of Arhdeacon Williams with a view to your visiting the district of Ahuriri, etc, and any other places in that neighbourhood that the Archdeacon may suggest. You will receive his suggestions as to the best mode of obtaining from the natives a grant of land, not exceeding 10 acres, for a Mission Station and Chapel. . . The land must be as near as possible to the principal *pa*, and probably will be the exact spot pointed out to me by the chiefs when I visited the place last year.' There followed a long list of places across the country, which Colenso was to visit, 'and bring me back a circumstantial account of the number and statement of the inhabitants.' To this was appended a disciplinary pill: 'I have already explained the mode in which I wish your Catechetical services to be conducted, to distinguish them from those of ordained Clergymen who have received license and Commission to preach.' Evidently Selwyn was bent on keeping Colenso in his place.

A little later an old Cornish family from the St Austell district, the Carlyons of Tregrehan, made an enormous purchase of land in this new unexplored area. A junior branch of the family established itself there, built a large country house and formed an estate named Guavas,[1] after one of their old Cornish properties. There they proceeded to live the life of the gentry at home—and ultimately succeeded to the senior line in Cornwall. I do not know if there grew up any relations between these two Cornish families in that vicinity—unlikely in any case after Colenso's downfall, though he was to spend the rest of his life in the area.

William landed at Ahuriri with his little family safely in December 1844. 'The exceedingly heavy toil of forming a new station among crowds of strange and heathen Maoris, combined with so much travelling imposed on me by the Bishop—hundreds of miles rough and distant on foot during the year—brought on a serious attack of low fever. . . It was now past our midwinter; very cold and wet we found it in our unfinished *raupo* hut, and on the wet ground in a low and swampy situation.'

William's wife was in an advanced state of pregnancy again (the disadvantageous pregnability of women!) 'There was no medical man nor European woman in those parts, and she feared the result, having suffered severely and long on the birth of her first child, Fanny.' They decided to travel up to Poverty Bay, to Archdeacon Williams' kind home, as nearest place of help. 'But how to get there was the difficulty—at this season in particular it made one shudder to think of.' William had reason to reflect, as I always have done—he travels fastest who travels alone, without impedimenta.

1. This means low-lying winter pasture.

'No time, however, was to be lost, so we three—Mrs C., Fanny and myself started on foot, I so weak from my late fever as to be scarcely able to walk and Mrs C. in her almost dangerous state for such a journey.' Their Maoris carried the baby, and sometimes trundled the mother over the beaches or level ground in a kind of hand-barrow. At length they reached haven, but William could remain only a day or two: he had the journey back to make all over again, as he had to do the setting up of the new station, where all the goods and stores were expected. Elizabeth had with her as nurse-girl, Ripeka, christened Rebecca, a Maori of good class from the boarding-school at Waimate. A couple of days after William had left a son was born.

His wife wrote to him an account of this unhappy event, explaining that 'it would not be her fault if anything of that nature ever again occurred. For this I praised her (in my own mind), for it would be impossible as we then were situated—wholly isolated and cut off from useful help—to carry on our work as active missionaries and to have a quickly increasing family. I had seen evidence of that evil in the North. So from that time, or long before, we never again cohabited as man and wife.'

Summer was advanced before wife and children returned. Meanwhile William was travelling about on his duties, as was the indefatigable Bishop, whom he had to meet on his return from Wellington in the far South to Auckland in the North. He also had to conduct his lordship across the country half-way back, visiting new missions, the missionaries still in tents. On his little family's return he was able to baptize the new baby, now nearly six months old, 'giving him the honoured, ecclesiastical name of Ridley Latimer, which alone would serve to show how I believed, and how deeply my heart and mind were set on my work.' A kind of manifesto in its way: it would also serve to show his High Church superior how irredeemably Protestant this individual missionary was.

As for his wife, 'we had hitherto had but little if any love for each other, and our new mode of living did not cause such a feeling to spring or grow.' William accepted it as best in the circumstances. 'My home was not in the dwelling house in the Mission Station. My happiness was *in my work* among the

Maoris, which was everywhere growing and prospering, in spite of great opposition from the powerful heathen chiefs, and other sources. Mrs Colenso was evidently far happier when I was away from the Station travelling. She too had a heart for her work in the girls' and infants' schools, in which she did good service—and was always an excellent mother to her children.' William, too, was happier away travelling, roughing it with his Maoris.

The ground he had to cover in the course of duty, under Archdeacon Williams' charge, was almost one quarter of North Island, and it involved ceaseless journeys. In spite of the hardships and dangers—William had no head for heights and was apt to be sea-sick—he was happy in these, happy in his work with the Maoris, as authoritative in his sphere with them as the Bishop was with everybody. Then there were the pleasures—reading the New Testament in Maori to the natives, who delighted in myths and folk tales. He does not seem to have been confronted with the awkward questions about them which 'the intelligent Zulu' raised with his cousin in Natal. But there were plenty of other confrontations and difficulties in the relations between races. One of his women servants had been separated from her husband by her chief. Colenso protested; the chief retaliated by charging her with adultery with one of the Station boys. The boy confessed to misdemeanour, but with another woman. 'This trend in native morality, a result of the clash of differing standards, required compensation from Colenso, whose employee was the guilty party.'

When he refused to pay the *utu* (damages) demanded, the enraged chief, a big powerful type, manhandled him, pummelling his head on the ground. Thereupon William demanded *utu*. The natives dared not intervene against their chief, so William upbraided them all in fluent Maori, reminding them that there was scarcely one of them who had not received some benefit from him, while he was wearing himself out in their service. In chapel next day they were dressed down on the text, 'Touch not mine anointed, and do my prophets no harm.'

The adultery charge came before him to adjudicate. When the girl admitted that she had no charge to lay against anyone,

the chiefs who had backed her wrapped their faces in their
mats, got up and went away. Colenso wept with relief, and
gave judgment that the girl should live with her husband. 'The
deflated party shortly returned with a large canoe, which was
voluntarily handed over as *utu* for the false accusation.' All's
well that ends well.

At the Mission Station he was happy in what he called his
'study', really a little cottage on his own out in the garden,
where he was available for his Maori menfolk, could arrange
his collections and was for ever writing. With his addiction to
detail we know what his cottage and the life he led there was
like. 'A two-roomed cottage, wholly floored with *kauri*, its
ornamentation was an exercise for the most talented native
craftsmanship available. The frame was of old dark *totara*
laboriously dug from the bed of the Tukituki some miles
distant. . . Here he usually slept . . . here he dried and
mounted his specimens, packing them with infinite care and
exhaustive notes for despatch to the Hookers.' Here he did his
writing, conducting a large correspondence, keeping up his
journals, reporting on his activities to the C.M.S.—whom he
looked to as his real superiors, rather than the Bishop, for they
paid his salary, and there was a certain jealousy between those
two authorities. The 'study' was his work-place, 'a refuge
where his exile became a real happiness.'

All round, garden and orchard were being planted up, seeds
and roots arriving, his few cattle looked after—fresh milk
supply (we do not hear of Cornish cream being made as at
Bishopstowe). All this gave employment to the Maoris, casual
as they were, not broken in to regular work Western-style.

This, and the taboo-ridden nature of their age-old society,
led to many absurdities; often irritated, William does not seem
to have appreciated their absurd side. Road-making was a
prime priority; and over some dispute about building a
boatshed a local chief declared the road to the Station taboo,
which of course held up all traffic. William thereupon placed
on it 'a kitchen boiler for cooking pork, which once more made
the road *noa* (common).' This might have led to a *fracas*, but he
had already left on one of his journeys.

On one of these across the mountains an old chief imparted
the information that an attack he had intended on Hawke's

Bay was frustrated by one of his men peeing on a sacred mountain top—and that would have incurred defeat for the expedition. The old boy was furious when Colenso told him that he had already stood on that sacred spot. He was warned not to commit further desecration by following that route.

In an attempt to cross a mountain desert in a snowstorm William's native guide refused to go further. At one time seventy men had been lost there, and William himself was held responsible for the bad weather. 'Murmurs throughout this wretched long and dreary day reached my ears—of my having been the means of bringing on this weather! through my uprooting some small trees (*dacrydiums*), my crossing the desert without observing certain superstitious ceremonies, and my sacrilegiously eating some *gaultheria* berries while crossing, which the guide had detected!!'

Crossing these deserts, tracts of scoria, volcanic ash, or the numerous shingly beaches on routes along the coast, was very hard on Western feet—apparently the natives walked better by turning in their toes. There were too frequent rivers and streams to cross in those beautiful gorges; often the track involved crossing the same stream from side to side dozens of times.

Happily in good weather or bad there were the consolations of the flora. Emerging from forest and shrub on the inland approach to Hawke's Bay, 'on to open dell-like land, the lovely appearance of so many varied, beautiful and novel wild plants and flowers richly repaid *me* the toil of the journey and the ascent. Never before did I behold at one time such a profusion of Flora's stores! I was overwhelmed and stood looking with all my eyes, greedily devouring and drinking in the enchanting scene before me.'

Everywhere he went he was collecting—many of them novelties. Here two new ferns, *alsophila colensoi* and *hypolepis millefolium*; there *taramea* or *acyphilla*, circled by needle-sharp leaves. 'One of the most striking of his discoveries was the New Zealand edelweiss, *leucogenes leontopodium*, "a little shrubby plant which scarcely seemed like a living plant at all, being so dry and sapless and densely woolly." ' Every trip produced new finds. The shrub *senecio greyii*—evidently named for the famous Governor, Sir George Grey—'favoured today by

many gardeners', originally belonged to the coastline of Palliser Bay in the extreme South. No naturalist myself, it is
pleasant to find his name attached to his finds, *hebe colensoi*
among others; the books are full of his discoveries—I cite only
a few examples from them. The Maoris, knowing this strange
man's passion for these things, would bring rarities from
remote places to his study, among them alpines from the high
Ruahine Range, which excited him with the desire to
penetrate it one day.

He was acquainted with the splendid spectacle of high
Mount Edgcumbe—named for another of the Cornish families
pioneering in the new country. In this case the New Zealand
branch of that historic family succeeded to the peerage at
home, as the Carlyons of Hawke's Bay succeeded to the
ancestral estate in Cornwall. On one journey into the interior
Colenso called at the remote mission conducted by a Cornish
Wesleyan, the Rev. J. Buller. Another of that family made a
survey of New Zealand bird-life. The Taranaki district in the
south-west below New Plymouth was settled largely from
Cornwall and Devon. One finds their place names on the map:
Pencarrow Head, on the way south to upheaved Cook Strait,
comes from the estate of the Molesworths, who contributed
their brightest specimen, well-known Sir William, to colonial
affairs as Secretary of State.

As time went on there developed a notable traffic in plants
and seeds, since the climate of Cornwall turned out to be
suitable for New Zealand vegetation. Cornish gentry and
gardeners—Boscawens, Tremaynes, Bolithos, Williamses—all
took a hand, the Carlyons a leading part, in acclimatising New
Zealand flora, which Cornish gardens now display in all their
finery. One's only regret is that the Cornish there have not had
the enterprise to write up their contribution to the fascinating
new country at the other end of the world.

As a good Celt Colenso often thought of his favourite poet,
Ossian, on his journeys, identifying himself with that voice
from Highland fastnesses: 'It is night. I am alone, forlorn on
the hill of storms. The wind is heard on the mountain. The
torrent pours down the rock. No hut receives me from the rain,
forlorn on the hill of winds.' The climate, like the Highlands of
Scotland, or Cornwall—all the Celtic lands—was rainy, and

often we read of him sopping-wet as he marched, usually ahead of his bearers, scouting for plants; or dossing down for the night in a mud-swamped hut. In his little book, *In Memoriam*, he says, let anyone who doubts these trials 'try a run with a load on his back *over the rocks* from the mouth of the river at Manawarakau to Pauanui: or *over the rocks* from Akitio to Owahanga; or the tramp by the strict coast-line from Cape Palliser to Wellington.' One sees settlements, and the missions, extending now all the way from the extreme north to Wellington at the bottom of the Island, on Cook Strait—it does not appear that Colenso crossed over.

No love was lost between settlers and missionaries. Colenso opposed the incomers from squatting on native lands. The Church had a good record in this regard, doing what it could to protect the Maoris' interests. Even one of the official McLean's agents, 'Maori Jim' Grindell, declared: 'one reason I have against the Missionary is that formerly, before these wretches took to psalm-singing, a man could get a pig and a woman at every place free, but now it is just the reverse.' The large Hawke's Bay area had more natives than most and, unreached as yet by white administration, was more lawless. As for the incoming settlers, one reporter described them as 'the very lowest and worst he ever knew—runaway soldiers and man-o'-wars-men, convicts from New South Wales and Van Diemen's land, who openly boast of their defiance of the government.' Colenso was between the devil and the deep sea, sometimes involved in fisticuffs with natives, with whom he took a high hand as the children they were. Then the weather took a high hand with him, and in the swampy situation of the mission he was flooded out. A local chief commiserated him 'no-one ever lived here on this spot before you: it has been only the dwelling place of the eel.' The swollen river flooded his cottage, the sea rose over the high bank in front of the house; after the storm subsided, 'only the swiftly rushing ripple of the current as it shot past, the faint snorting of a drowning pig.'

It would seem that in this new rough area, where the white settlers thoroughly unsettled the natives and set them the worst example, Colenso was caught between the two. His biographers conclude that his 'regimented and exacting Christianity imposed too heavy a strain on the recently converted', who, encouraged by hostile chiefs, began to fall away. I find him taking too uncompromising a line about sexual morals, in the high Victorian manner, and that was to find him out.

Chapter III
Downfall: the Crisis

From the end of 1851 and throughout 1852 and 1853 the threads and themes of Colenso's life tangled themselves into a knot, which took a great deal of undoing. He tells us that as a boy in Cornwall an old woman used to say to him when in trouble, 'it can't be helped, you were born under a malignant planet.' I have observed before that the Colensos had more than their share of ill luck.

At the same time the future of the whole Hawke's Bay area was determined. In principle the government only had the right to purchase land from the chiefs, at this time ready to sell—they were not making use of much of it—for good money. The government Commissioner, Donald McLean, a commanding figure, arrived to put through the first sales of large blocks in the area. Colenso was saddened to see this happening under his eyes. 'Now I am asked to counsel you to sell your land to the Government, but I tell you candidly I cannot do so. I shall not now deviate from what I have always told you— Never to part with the whole of your land: and, when you part with any, be sure to have a good natural boundary between.' On 17 November 'Ahuriri, so long coveted, has also passed into the hands of the foreigner: the price £1500, of which £1000 has also been paid down in gold!! *Sic transit gloria mundi aut Novae Zelandiae*!! Already a big block at Hapuku had been sold—I do not know whether one or other of these constituted the original Carlyon holding of some 30,000 acres.

Land purchase, sentimentalism apart, meant agricultural progress and material improvement for the natives. 'Hundreds of bushels of wheat were raised annually from the seed procured originally by Colenso, while the annual value of exports from native labour evidenced the growing industry of Kahungunu—the local tribesmen. Horses were among the most valued imports; their chief, Renata—with whom Colenso sometimes clashed—became a horse-dealer.

McLean himself formed a good opinion of the resident missionary and the work he was doing: 'such a straight-forward excellent man. I have a great respect for him. [He] has given me many interesting accounts of his experiences among the natives and of his various narrow escapes, and determined proceedings with them, conquering their obstinacy and violent passions.' McLean reported him to be 'a zealous, conscientious man and an excellent devoted missionary, well entitled to support from the Government. He certainly deserves the utmost consideration being given to his plans [for large native reserves, giving them security], as he has really worked a wonderful change on the natives of this place.' However, there was another side to the missionary's life which the Commissioner was not to know.

Colenso's closest attendants were his steward, Hamuera, baptized Samuel; and Ripeka, Mrs Colenso's nurse-girl, Christian name Rebecca. Colenso was much opposed to their marrying, though he may have had to perform the ceremony they went through—who else was there to do it? He certainly did not want to lose them from his service. Hamuera had been with him for some seventeen years, having been rescued as a small boy, a mere slave, from being killed and eaten. When he was taken in by Colenso he was in a frightful state from scrofula—holes in neck, breast, and armpits—and then 'perfectly cured by God's blessing on the means' (decent food, I suspect). Ripeka was even more indispensable.

At the end of May she gave birth to a boy, expressing pleasure at the child's light colour: 'Aue! he pakeha!' (white man). Mrs Colenso brought the child over to her husband in his cottage-study, exclaiming, 'Ekite, Neo, a fine boy.' She is supposed not to have suspected, but women are always aware in such matters. The boy was to be called Willie.

William had a good enough alibi had he chosen, for Ripeka was married to Hamuera, and in a short time was pregnant again with *his* child. However, women usually tell each other, even if William remained silent. In the account he gave to this son of the circumstances of his birth—still shamefaced and self-accusing many years after, as an old man he says naively, 'Rebecca was always very very kind and willing to do anything for me at all times day or night—particularly when in pain—

and ever without murmur or cross look. Indeed she was a merry laughing soul, the idol of the two children and the light in our house. And so the connection (!) between us took place.'

She must indeed have provided a welcome contrast to Mrs C., unwilling and—to judge from her photograph—rather a ramrod. 'Of the relationship Mrs C. knew all about it very soon after the child's birth, at which she had kindly assisted—as Rebecca had never once been told by me to keep anything secret.' Elizabeth was much taken with the new baby and looked after it as one of her own—here was the best side to her, along with her stalwart work for the Mission and School.

Leaving this pretty kettle of fish boiling behind him–and the situation unresolved—William took off for a mountain journey through the Ruahine Range, penetrating from the northern end. The fine forests of fagus had been much damaged by the frequent casual fires of the natives, but there were the consolations of botanising, a respite from growing worry. 'Here in this ruined spot of burnt sticks one of Flora's graceful children, a fine and lovely clematis, the New Zealand harbinger of spring, had sprung up and twined to the top of one of the smaller trees, displaying its elegant blossoms waving in the wind. Even my native companions burst into exclamations of astonishment at the beauty of the flowers, which here in this miserable place spoke a language intelligible to all our hearts.'

Weather was bad, snow on the heights; sometimes a stream had to be crossed with William borne on the back of one of his upstanding bearers. I don't think he was a big man, or a heavyweight: he was sometimes knocked down in a dispute with a Maori chief, when the men dared not intervene—taboo!

Arrived at a snow-bound village, he observed the large *kowhai* trees, *edwardsia grandiflora*: these were covered with their golden flowers and mostly without leaves. 'The sun was shining brightly, and the parrots flocked screaming from the forest to the blossoms. It was a strange sight to see them, how deftly they managed to go out to the end of a long lithe branch and there swinging, back downwards, lick out the honey with their big tongues, without injuring the young fruit.' With his professional eye he observed how it was done minutely, and describes it as usual in too much detail.

In the native village, 'poor creatures, at this season they

were all living on fern root, which the children were incessantly roasting and hammering. Yet they were all very healthy. Cook's early statement of their being a remarkably healthy race I have often found to be true. Would that the introduction of European habits and of "civilisation" had not deprived them of that blessing.'

As normal humans what they liked of European civilisation was horse-racing, card-playing, and drink. Horses, of course, were a novelty, and William was shocked to find the horse-racing taking place around chapel and burying ground. Strait-laced Evangelical as he was, he expressed his displeasure to the offenders. There were moral lapses in the congregation to be inquired into. He severely reproved the offenders and passed judgment: some were excluded from school, others had to pay compensation. He made a politic decision, since there were people living together unmarried, that if a couple wished to cohabit, and had their parents' consent, the native preacher might publish the banns; they might then live together as man and wife, and when Colenso came round again he would marry them.

On his return he packed up his specimens from this trip to Sir William Hooker at Kew, reporting that he 'will find so many bad, half-rotten and imperfect, that his opinion of me will not, I fear, be improved thereby. But I have done what I could and shall, I believe, henceforward be almost necessitated to give up the *work*—for such I now find it to be: quite enough, *alone*, fully to employ any one person.' From this it would appear that he must have been employed by Hooker, and would have received some remuneration to supplement his miserable allowance as a missionary.

There were compensations. Sir William sent him botanical books—his son's work on Sikkim Rhododendrons, for example. Here was another admirable consequence of the forward march of Victorian expansion—expeditions into the Himalayas, Nepal, Burma, Malaya, as well as South America, to bring back and propagate rare trees and plants. In these areas a famous pair of Cornishmen, the Lobb brothers, made their mark, financed by an Exeter nursery and West Country supporters.

'I am still collecting, and I hope to add much yet to the *Algae* and smaller *Crypts*. I have also a few *new* things among the phanerogamous plants—a very pretty and altogether unique *veronica*, a small shrub having glaucescent serrated leaves and flowering in the early spring; a ranunculus or two, another *exarrhena*, ditto *myosotis* or two, and some *orchideae*; and a *hymenophyllum*, which has pleased me much, a species allied to *H. Wilsoni*.' He hoped to send all these after the present busy season, 'as the *whole* of my *summer time* is *fully occupied* in travelling throughout an extensive parish larger than some English counties.'

On his return there were other things to occupy him. First thing that fell to him was to investigate a charge of adultery before a large concourse of natives. 'His decision in favour of the accused husband gave general satisfaction, except to the wife. "To me it was a most grievous spectacle to see her using all her powers to ruin the teacher of the village and father of her five children." ' One wonders what the natives were thinking, or what himself, with his own ruin impending. He does not seem to have appreciated the irony in regard to his own case—people don't.

In the midst of all this the Bishop arrived on his visitation, more sharp-eyed and worn with his life of unceasing exertion and travel. He had come overland from Wellington and, weary and footsore, stayed a week. Plenty of time for Colenso to come up against Authority personified—and no Colenso had much liking for authority, except his own.

Selwyn noticed at once a few more cattle about the place than he had bound the deacon to keep. Colenso retorted that he couldn't prevent his cows calving. The reply annoyed his lordship. William justified himself by saying that milk was distributed daily to the Maoris, and that he had tried to get surplus cattle removed to Auckland or Wellington. The Bishop regarded Colenso's injunctions against games and horse-races as too strict, and produced a letter of protest from the new Catholic priest in the district against him. William took this up with 'this fellow'; the High Church prelate said he could not sit at table with one who called a priest a 'fellow'. (No doubt about *Catholic* orders!)

Colenso raised the question of the infrequent administration of Communion. The Bishop said he knew what Colenso

was aiming at—priest's orders. Well he might. He had served
seven years as a deacon, and ten years before that at C.M.S.
work. Selwyn believed that his reports to the C.M.S. were
unfriendly to him. This Colenso indignantly denied. Anyway,
it was usual for a deacon to proceed to priesthood after a year.
He had seen the young men from the university, whom the
Bishop brought out with him, made priests with none of his
own experience and record in the mission field. Now Selwyn
came half-way to meet him and, informing him that he
intended to ordain him priest that September, ordered him to
meet him at Otaki for the purpose. Colenso said hotly that he
had determined never to accept priesthood at his hands.

Once before they had clashed on this subject. Colenso had
pointed out that his Christian converts had noticed the
infrequency of the 'Last Supper'—an Evangelical term that
could not have recommended him to Selwyn, who had
quashed him haughtily, 'Seek ye the priesthood also?' Some of
the natives were cute enough to call William a 'half-minister'.
When he ran into the Bishop accidentally in Wellington,
Selwyn wanted to know what he was doing there—when he
had gone there on the Bishop's direction to visit two *pas* on the
North Shore of Cook Strait. William was invited to dine with
Dr Featherstone in the evening; when he found that the Bishop
was to be there, he made off at once to the *pa* where his tent
was standing. It is pretty clear that, where his lordship was
accustomed to submission, these two jarred on each other.

Undoubtedly William had an inferiority complex, and no
tact—but an inferiority complex often goes with a sense of
superiority within. William knew his own quality, and that no
one's work in the field had surpassed his. Today, looking back
over his career as a whole, we can say that no record quite
equalled his for the uniqueness of his personality; the
distinctiveness of his double contribution to New Zealand as
missionary and botanist, and the story of notable Cornishmen
around the world.

The Bishop was hard at work with his duty, confirming over
100 natives whom Colenso had prepared for the rite ('je ne
vois pas la nécessité'). Then the two left together for the
overland route, Colenso accompanying his superior as usual
part of the way. 'We got late, nearly midnight, to Waikari, we

two alone, hungry and tired, ahead of our poor laden baggage bearers [episcopal gear!] who could not keep up with us. There we were glad to sit in a little *whare* [hut] with nothing to eat and patiently await their arrival.'

In the morning the Bishop softened, and said that his heart rejoiced at what he had seen all through Colenso's large district, the best Mission of all—when he was disheartened elsewhere, including his own school at Auckland where things were not going well. He greatly wished that William would re-consider his decision and accept priest's orders, and thereupon 'gave me his Episcopal benediction. And so we parted, never more to meet on friendly or good terms.'

During his stay Selwyn had shown the kindlier side to his nature, often taking the baby Willie on his knee with 'What a fine boy.' But not a word was said of the problem in the background. William had it on the tip of his tongue to make a full confession, but was put off by the lack of sympathy between them. Mrs Colenso said nothing.

When he returned the storm broke, and lashed him on all sides. Ripeka had turned against him and told all to her tribesmen, who naturally took her side. She and her husband now wanted to leave Colenso for good and return to native life; but, with her child by Hamuera dying—duly buried by Colenso—she wanted to take her child by him away with her. Things would have been better for him, at least far easier to smooth over, if he had been prepared to allow this. Obstinately he clung to the child, determined to bring it up as his own. Conflict of wills raged fiercely, and at last the couple prepared to abscond by canoe, smuggling the child with them. Only at the last moment was he snatched back, and the couple left without him—to organise sympathy, in other words make trouble with their people.

It is difficult to sort out all the complications, though we can follow the consequences that ensued. At one point the local chief, Tipuna, summoned the missionary—*mana* much diminished—to account. William went to meet a concourse of natives, expecting to be killed—and apparently willing enough, as a way out of his difficulties. On a subsequent occasion he came into conflict with Tipuna, who laid a charge that William had kicked him.

The missionary was had up before the first formal court to
be held there, no longer 'the honoured authority and arbitra-
tor' he had been for years past, 'but as a pre-judged defendant
in a charge of common asault.' Tipuna gave evidence before
the assembled natives, and produced 'the knife which the
missionary had offered him.' The Bench gave judgment
against him, £3. 'The Rev. W. Colenso said that he would not
pay the £3, or even 6d.' All very well to be obstinate and hold
out *contra mundum*, but it was all the more humiliating.

He had no sympathy whatever from his own white men: they
were arrayed against him for his opposing the purchase of
native lands, even those of friendly McLean under government
authority.

Now Elizabeth's family was to take a hand. Finally, there
was the Bishop to confront.

Things were tumbling about William's ears. I get the
impression that he was losing his nerve.

Unknown to her husband Mrs Colenso had written to her
family, and one morning her brother, John Fairburn, suddenly
descended upon them. 'John stayed with us some time; I told
him *all* that had taken place and intimated what I might
(possibly) have to prepare for, if dealt with harshly.' Evidently,
at this point, William had no clear idea what the future might
hold. 'John behaved very kindly and quite won my heart,
saying that I should never want a friend and that I could reside
with him, etc, etc.'

'It was arranged that John was to take his sister's two
children away with him to be placed at school at Auckland.
This was in every way proper, because neither of them *spoke*
English, though both could read it, Maori being used by all of
us in the house.' William drafted his letter to the Bishop,
which Elizabeth and John approved, who was to deliver it
personally, 'and to tell him certain things on my behalf.'

When Selwyn returned from his tour of the South Sea
Islands, the poor man was presented with the unwelcome
news—one more headache. 'I believe the Bishop was greatly
moved, perhaps very angry. Unfortunately he examined
John—perhaps frightened him, John being a quiet, unsophisti-
cated colonial-born young man, who had spent most of his
years in the country.' John told all, and rather more than all,

that he knew: no attenuating circumstances. Perhaps he went over to the other side—these things happen. Elizabeth understandably did so. She had behaved very well through all these trying months; she had done her best to look after the child and protect him in the tug-of-war waged over his head. Her case reminds me of Lady Byron's, who behaved well enough over her husband's bad behaviour—until she got back to her own family, when she turned relentlessly against him. Elizabeth's behaviour was consistent—anyway, she was not emotionally involved: she and William had never had any affection for each other. Thus Ripeka had taken her place. . .

'The Bishop *immediately* called together a few clergymen—of his own friends, not one of mine among them—and laid before them my letter. They condemned me offhand at once. The Bishop *the same day* acted upon it, and issued his letter of suspension. The one thing I had begged of the Bishop was *not to act thus but to see me first*, for the sake of the Maoris—the rising Church; that the fact was well known here and they had long known it. If he wished it I would leave at once for Auckland to see him. But the blow was struck!'

Evidently William had not expected to be turned out like that in the cold.

It now remained to pick up the bits and pieces.

Nature also now took a hand to add to everybody's difficulties—the mess made by so little a thing. The mission house caught fire and burned down; one is reminded of the fire that destroyed Bishopstowe—and Colenso ill-luck. William rescued what he could—books, guns, clothes–but it meant the loss of most of his personal property. This was succeeded by the usual flooding of the river on that low swampy site.

The 'study', William's cottage, was unharmed, but must have been uncomfortable in every sense when the Bishop descended on them to pick up the pieces. No mercy for William: Selwyn must have felt justified in the mistrust he had always manifested for this recalcitrant character. He was to leave the premises and the district, and he would never be restored to the church. The child Willie was to be handed back to Ripeka.

This was precisely what William had resisted all along and brought the fuss into the open—made a public scandal out of what could have been kept a private matter—as we should regard it today. But this was the Victorian world, if in the Antipodes. William resisted all along the line, as might be expected of him: the wrangle went on and on in the damp cottage, floor covered with mud. He would *not* leave; he had nowhere to go to, and much of the improvements on the place had come from his own personal efforts and savings. He had one card to play: he was the employee of the Church Missionary Society; he would abide by their decision, not the Bishop's.

Poor Selwyn now came up with a suggestion in what he considered to be the interest of 'that dear child'—leaning across William to kiss the boy, whose charm everybody seems to have succumbed to. Mrs Colenso was to take him to her parents, the Fairburns at Auckland, who would bring him up. She agreed, and the scene ended with the episcopal bene-diction upon William's head—though that had not been the offending member; 'Unto God's gracious mercy and protec-tion we commit thee.' When he rode off next morning he did not speak to William.

The episcopal solution regarding the baby did not work. Elizabeth was willing enough, looked after the baby on the trek to Auckland, reporting almost daily to William on its well-being, etc. When she got home to her parents they would not, however, take charge. In William's account of these happen-ings, written for his son many years after as a grown man— then married to his cousin in Cornwall—he paid tribute to his wife's 'kind, extra-motherly care of the infant . . . more than words can express. . . and I shall never forget it.'

Eventually the boy was handed over to his Maori grand-parents at the Bay of Islands, and his father desolated did not see him again for another eight years. 'Often indeed had I vainly tried to get you brought to me, offering large rewards; but on every occasion I was hindered and frustrated by the folk, our enemies, in the North—and all done under the guise of religion. I could relate a good deal more of what followed', he added to the account, 'of persecutions and insults and of patient abiding; of troubles and trials and severe losses. And this further relation I may yet give you.' He seems never to have had the time, or perhaps the heart, to go over it all—but he certainly developed what today would be regarded as a persecution complex.

Early next year, 1854, Alfred Domett the poet, who devoted such time as he could spare from writing a long epic to being Commissioner of Crown Lands, arrived to lay out the new town of Napier, where William eventually made his home—for, *pace* the Bishop, he would not leave the neighbourhood. He would live on there, long outliving Selwyn, to face out his disgrace, ostracised by the Church. He would make a new life.

Domett found him most helpful: 'really of great use, though I find he is an overbearing and rather cantankerous fellow *among the natives*. To *me* he is over-polite and painfully obliging.' His knowledge of the area was indispensable—still more so, funnily enough, over another case of adultery. Domett knew no Maori, and so William had to be called in, no longer to adjudicate but to advise. He reported it all to Elizabeth—not a ghost of a sense of humour, more likely a sense of self–justification: Victorians took these things so earnestly. Once more the ruined Mission station was flooded out—it was to be removed to a new site, with a newcomer in charge. On his return from the adultery proceedings, he reported to her, 'before I came to the church I found the flood up on the bank. I waded to the river's edge and spent nearly an hour in endeavouring to make old Matiaha hear, but in vain. At last I returned, headed the flood water, and came over the sea beach, intending to swim across with the key of the study in my mouth.' He had often enough had to do that kind of thing on his travels, crossing fords or swimming a flooded stream—nothing new. At last a white man sheltering in a deserted hut put him across in a cockle-shell of a dinghy in the half darkness. 'Leaping out, I waded to the study. Soon after the whole garden was flooded.'

From all points of view a new start in a new place was indicated. Fortunately for him, some time before a friendly chief had insisted on conferring upon him a small section of land, for himself personally, not for the Church or for any successor. Assembling what he could of his personal possessions, he sold them in Wellington, even his books, thus raising enough money for a new start in a small way. Self-help would be the line of rehabilitation. From the point of view of his biographers, for the next three years he went under: nothing is known of his activities, and from him—normally so given to verbiage—never a word.

He must have undergone a dark night of the soul—to emerge a changed man.

Chapter IV

Recovery. Public Career

Even in the worst years after his downfall Colenso did not
wholly go under—unlike the very first of the missionaries,
Thomas Kendall, who went native. He is celebrated in a fine
poem by Keith Sinclair—a rare combination of historian and
poet: 'Memorial to a Missionary',

> Instructed to speak of God with emphasis
> On sin and its consequence, to cannibals
> Of the evil of sin, he came from his father's farm,
> The virtuous home, the comfortable chapel. . .
>   The scurrilous sailors spoke
> More clearly with rum and lusting, so he turned
> To the native vowels for symbols, sought to make
> The World of God anew, in the tribes' first book
> Laying in Christ's advance a path of nouns.

So far that spoke for Colenso too; but not so much what
followed in Kendall's case:

> He drank the waters of the underworld
> Lying all day in the unconverted flesh
> Entangled in old time, before Christ's birth,
> Beyond redemption, found what a nest of bliss,
> A hot and mushroom love lay fair in the fern. . .

Still, something of Kendall's fate fell on Colenso:

> The unfaithful shepherd was sent from the farm of souls
> To live, a disgraceful name in the Christian's ear,
> A breathing sin among the more tolerant chiefs.

William did not fall so far as that: he kept along with his own
white people, though ostracised by the Church.

135

Old friends forsook him—notably his best friend in early days, Archdeacon Williams, now on his way to becoming one of Selwyn's bishops. They considered that William had disgraced the Church—in the heavy way in which Victorians regarded sexual lapses. Oddly enough, apart from the Ripeka affair, William doesn't seem to have had any further to-do with sex—rough luck that *that* brief affair should have led to so much trouble. The clerics not only turned against him but became hostile—notably Williams, as we shall see.

Celts are notoriously touchy and resentful—and, when wounded, are liable to get their own back. This is what happened with William–not very Christian of him: his cousin, the Bishop of Natal, did not react like that, and he had a great deal to put up with. He was morally superior to William or, for that matter, to almost anyone—rather a saint.

I find William's reaction psychologically more interesting. Cast out by the Church, he went over to the settlers: they were laymen, they took his mishap more charitably and did not hold it against him. He could make his life with them—and a better livelihood than as an impecunious missionary, dependent on the whim of Church Missionary Society and Bishop Selwyn. Moreover, a new start was in keeping with his fundamental nature, the natural man, his spirit of independence, his Cornish individualism. (As far as that goes, he was a prime case.)

He turned his back on the sacrifices he had made for the Church, the constant hand-outs to the Maoris. He did not cease to be charitable and even generous; but henceforth his interests were those of a settler, though he did not hesitate to speak up for the Maoris when he thought right. As for the settlers, Keith Sinclair puts their situation with the conciseness of verse, in his poem '1859':

> We need a harbour where the breakers melt,
> We need a doorway that our ships may leap
> From the sides of the possessive land
> Against the resistant bars of the great waves,
>
> And fields without one black barbaric tree;
> Meadows, and a harbour to the abjured past,
> To build a people nearer to our needs
> In the unbaked clay, the unconsecrated waste.

For Colenso the past was not wholly abjured, but henceforth his work would lie in helping to build up a dominion for his own 'nearer' white people.

New Zealand itself was changing fundamentally. From the year 1858 the whites for the first time became more numerous than the Maoris—who still held the bulk of the land, and could not make the best of it. The increasing number of immigrants meant increasing pressure for land for proper settlement. Until the outbreak of the Maori wars in the 1860s the natives in fact were more prosperous than before—with money coming to them, economic expansion, increase of trade, a useful degree of inflation. A powerful and experienced Governor, Sir George Grey, had maintaied the general principle of governmental control of land purchase, but greatly lowered the price. Settlers poured in.

For some years he opposed their demand for 'responsible government'—as did Bishop Colenso in Natal—really in the interest of the natives. Grey's first period of rule, 1845—1853, was a benevolent autocracy—best in the circumstances. In 1853 he became Governor of Cape Colony, where he gained the confidence of the Kaffirs. (*Then* even the Orange Free State favoured federation with the Cape. The Colonial Office, by a malevolent fate, opposed it.) Grey came back to New Zealand for a second term of office in 1861, which turned out far less happily.

Meanwhile the institutions of a modern democratic state were coming into being—provincial Councils and a General Assembly for the amenities of discussion and debate, a kind of Parliament (Carlyle's 'talking shop') to hamper Grey's administration.

Such was the background to the second half of Colenso's life, and in these developments he took some considerable part. He lived so long, right up to 1899, that he may be said to have seen the whole saga through.

Three years passed in silence and solitude. But it seems to me that William Colenso was always a solitary man, unlike his cousin in Natal. The Bishop had the inner support of an utterly happy family life, and friends. Nothing of this for William. For a few years he had his wife's help in the mission

work, but that was all—no affection, then there was Ripeka—
no friends to speak of. He was happiest out in the wilds in that
beautiful country, tramping ahead of his native bearers looking for flowers. He certainly had a sense of beauty—no
evidence that the upright Bishop had.

His acquaintance, Alfred Domett (1811–1887),—earliest of
New Zealand poets—expressed these pleasures in verse.

> And thus o'er many a mountain wood-entangled,
> And stony plain of stunted fern that hides
> The bright green oily anise; and hill sides
> And valleys, where its dense luxuriance balks
> With interclinging fronds and tough red stalks
> The traveller's hard-fought path—they took their way.
> Sometimes they traversed, half the dreary day,
> A deep-glenned wilderness all dark and dank
> With trees, whence tattered and dishevelled dangled
> Pale streaming strips of mosses long and lank;
> Where at each second step of tedious toil
> On forms of fallen trunks moss-carpeted,
> Perfect to every knot and bole, they tread,
> And ankle-deep sink in their yielding bed
> Of rottenness for ages turned to soil. . .

This was the so familiar inland scene; then on the coast:

> Or else on sands that, white and loose, give way
> At every step, they toil; till labour-sped
> Their limbs in the noon loneliness they lay
> On that hot, soft, yet unelastic bed
> With brittle seaweed, pink and black o'erstrown,
> And wrecks of many a forest growth upthrown,
> Bare stem and barkless branches, clean, sea-bleached,
> Milk-white—or stringy logs deep-red as wine,
> Their ends ground smooth against a thousand rocks.

The scene is no less recognisable. Domett, another Johnian
from Cambridge, was an interesting character, well-travelled
in America and Canada, at home a friend of Browning. In New
Zealand he got into politics, and was even Premier for a short

interval, 1862–3, during the Maori wars. As an official earlier, he was attacked as unorthodox in religion.

Colenso came to his defence. 'Now I should like to know, even believing that C. is a "religious" man and D. an "atheist", what has such to do with the matter of a *fit* man as Member of Council or Superintendent? Am I again to hear that any man is fit to govern a free and rising people *because* he is "religious"?. . Our long-looked-for July and August mails informed us of the breaking down of more of the barriers of superstitions and bigotry at home, in the admission of a Jew into Parliament.'

This was a new note from him. Evidently he had now emerged from the Evangelical strait-jacket in which he had been brought up. His troubles and trials had done that for him. By the end of 1857 he was able to offer a site at Napier, and a hefty donation, for a non-sectarian church, 'free for any Christian minister. . . I would also offer my own services gratuitously, i.e. to preach (D.V.) twice on the Sunday, and (if desired) once a week on some weekday evening; or assist any other minister whom they might select. And also take upon me to give a scientific lecture once a month throughout the same year.' One sees that he was not dis-interested: this suggestion—sensible in itself, when entertainments must have been few enough—was clearly a move to re-establish himself in the eyes of the growing community. No notice was taken of it.

However, he was becoming a man of property. He purchased a section in the rising town of Napier, and was able to advertise a 200 acre farm for letting. And he had other irons in the fire: a newspaper was set on foot, the *Hawke's Bay Herald*; he advised and instructed the printers. This was followed by the *Hawke's Bay Times*. Now regular contributions appeared from him in the papers— *Tracts for the Times*, on every current topic, mainly provincial politics, agriculture, growing apples rather than smoking tobacco. 'I want my countrymen to have something better on landing than to work on the roads, or to get a job in shearing the sheep of the few fortunate first comers. This may be very easily managed by "one and all" uniting in the work.'

'One and all' is of course the Cornish motto. He proposed that the Government should acquire the Ahuriri plains for agricultural purposes, granting land to intending farmers and also rations, if required, for the first year or so. He came to stand for the small farmer, as against the big pastoralists consigning large areas to sheep-runs. This was the dominant pattern in the even more mountainous South Island, depicted in the letters and books of Samuel Butler of *Erewhon*.

I see Colenso's Cornish background in his preference for the small farmer, for Cornwall is a country of small farms. His stand on this gave him votes when he stood for office, so that in 1859 he was elected Provincial Auditor or Treasurer, with a fair salary. The job involved a good deal of work, but we have seen that he was always a hard worker, and his work gave satisfaction. What it meant was that he was now an accepted public figure, respected by ordinary lay people, though still not by the Church. Thus, when the Taranaki war erupted, he was a government official and took a prudent course in regard to it.

In this country on the west coast there was good land for settled agriculture and white settlement lying waste along the Waitara river. But it was cursed by a feud between the local chief and a paramount chief, over a woman. A Maori saying has it: 'Women and land are the reasons why men die.' The local chief, to get his own back (over a woman!), sold the desirable land along that river, regardless of the claims of the head-chief and others. The government probably made a mistake in accepting the offer, not fully aware of the tangled situation between the Maoris. The perceptive Grey, away in Cape Town, seems to have spotted that there was a feud behind the eruption. The Maoris divided betwen sellers and non-sellers. The outbreak in this area sparked off a series of local wars in the 1860s.

Keith Sinclair tells us that 'New Zealand was intended to set the world an example of humane colonisation. The ideal was not attained. Racial relations soon came to resemble those on other frontiers. That the British Government failed to achieve its professed desire "to avoid, if possible, the disasters and the guilt of a sanguinary conflict with the native tribes", is no occasion for surprise: rather would it be a matter for astonishment if such wars, which seem everywhere to be part of the process of colonisation, had not occurred.'[1]

1. op. cit., 130 foll.

This strikes me as just, a real historian's judgment. In fact, at every juncture the sympathies of the Colonial Office were with the Maoris—but the Colonial Office was 12,000 miles away. Prior to the American Revolution—and one of the causes of it—the British Government at home wished to protect the American Indians from the ineluctable march of the colonists westward. But one cannot hold up the inevitable movements of history: one can only mitigate the sufferings— as Bishop Colenso so nobly did in South Africa.

And indeed in the Maori war there is much to remind one of that with the Zulus. 'For a time the Maoris had it all their own way. They had great courage, cunning and skill. They were born to fighting and enjoyed it. But their chief resource was the land . . . wild, hostile to the stranger, unsurveyed, and indeed mostly unexplored by the white man, the land was the Maori's ally. The Maoris had almost complete freedom of movement. They were not encumbered by baggage.' This reminds us of the Zulu *impi* that surprised the British encampment at Isandhlwana. Even the incapacity of the original commander in New Zealand, Colonel Gold, reminds one of the fumbling generals at the beginning of the Boer War.

'The Maori village at Waitara was burned by the troops, but the Maoris burned almost every farmhouse in Taranaki and captured most of the stock.' (This was the area of settlement from the old West Country: I should like to know what happened to the settlers—were they dispersed?) Thence the war spread—there developed a real Maori nationalism, with the election of a Maori King, in control of the mountainous interior—King Country—from which they could strike out in any direction. Maoris lapsed *en masse* from Christianity, some concocted a ghastly new compound, that of the Hau hau, who revived cannibalism. Their fanatical faith gave them extreme courage in battle; 'even the most practical demonstrations failed to convince the survivors that they had no magical protection against bullets.'

The war dragged on through the 1860s, spreading to the East Coast. The conflict became more bitter, marred by savagery. 'Missionaries were murdered. Prisoners were killed on both sides, eaten by one.' ('Long pig' as human flesh was described in Samoa, according to Robert Louis Stevenson.)

And, of course, the colonists were enthusiastic, all for war, as those in Natal were against the Zulus.

At the end of it all Maori power was broken as that of the Zulus was—worse, for, where the Zulus were left their land, 3 million acres of Maori land were confiscated. In practice they were permitted to keep half of this; all the same, the Colonial Office, helpless in the matter, was appalled by the measure. Sinclair describes it simply as 'a crime'.

Resistance to the inevitabilities of history usually speeds up the very process resistance was designed to halt. In England in 1536–7 the Pilgrimage of Grace, on behalf of the monasteries, only hastened the Dissolution of the greater ones.

All this must have been heart-breaking to Bishop Selwyn, whose sympathies were with the Maoris and against the land purchase at Waitara. He worked manfully to help sufferers and victims on both sides, in his dedicated way. During an interval in the war, in 1867, he returned to England for the Pan-Anglican Synod he had done much to promote. While there he was prevailed on, rather against his will, to retire on an English bishopric, after his life of inhuman exertion. He did not live to be an old man—Colenso survived his old opponent by twenty years. But Selwyn had done a great work—the real founder and organiser of the Church in New Zealand. I have no doubt he was a great man.

The result of the war was that henceforth the future of the country was in the hands of the white man. We cannot go into detail in the lingering struggle, flickering up, then dying down, like a forest fire. We must concentrate simply on how these developments affected Colenso, and what was his part in them. We can say that he was lucky to have been pushed out of the mission field before the war—he might well have been, in his exposed district, one of the missionaries to have been murdered. He was now in politics. We must see how that affected his attitude.

In 1861 he was elected to the General Assembly, in which he was not successful—too prolix, talking on any and every subject, instead of concentrating on one or two—the proper rule for Parliamentary success. And of course he was to be found in the ranks of the Opposition—I think he might fairly be described as 'Opposition-minded'. As warfare with the Maoris stepped up, and massacres ensued—one at Poverty Bay—the government brought in troops. Colenso opposed this measure; he was in favour of relying on the local militia and volunteers.

In 1865 he spoke out sympathetically for the Maoris, over the expedition to avenge the murder of a missionary, one Volkner. Colenso made the point that many had been killed who had had no part in the murder—and was himself attacked as a 'Philo-Maori'. In 1867 a band of raiders from the interior came down upon the coast at Napier. Colenso made a courageous offer to go out and meet them (as his cousin was to do in the Zulu war). He sent a message to McLean 'to offer you my personal services to go and see these unhappy people, to try and bring them to a better state of mind.' To no effect.

Two years later he made a public appeal 'for peace and forgiveness of native atrocities; that the war be immediately and everywhere stopped, a truce proclaimed . . . and commissioners appointed from both sides with full powers to settle equitably the questions between the two races.' No doubt he saw himself as one of them. He went on to attack the banishment of prisoners to the Chatham Islands as illegal. In the last year of the war one of the fiercest native leaders was captured—the Stone-age type who had eaten Volkner's eye. Colenso's old sympathies came out in a public plea for mercy. He argued that ample retribution had been inflicted, and proceeded to put the case of the wrongs the Maoris had suffered.

This was not appreciated by his former friend, Bishop Williams, who wrote: 'the evidence against him [the Chief] is as clear as possible, but an effort has been made by one person at Napier to show that he is not to be regarded as a guilty man and should receive a free pardon.' And again, 'we know well from what quarter this statement was made.' Colenso's plea was unsuccessful: the Chief was hanged.

The fact was that Williams had become an enemy. For years the Church authorities had been trying to push Colenso out of what was left of his old station at Waitangi, and he had doggedly refused—'dogged' was the word for him—until he received compensation for the improvements he had made.

After all, he had built his 'study', the cottage there. At last the Church people brought a court-case against him; they won, and a small fine was imposed on him.

At this opinion turned in his favour, and a wave of sympathy lapped round him at what his fellow townsmen regarded as victimisation. The Bishop wrote, 'Mr Colenso [not the *Rev.* Mr Colenso, as everybody else described him publicly] has been stirring up a demonstration in his favour among the élite of Napier. I hope that if this matter is brought before the House he will get the handling which he richly deserves. I mention for your information a few facts which may be of service. . .' Episcopal humbug—he proceeded to rake up the past. William replied reasonably that he was not actuated by any desire to retain Waitangi, though 'to me it is a place of many associations, pleasant and unpleasant, and time was when I could scarcely bear the loss of it.' His petition was supported by all the leading members of the community, laymen of course.

Bishop Williams returned to the charge. 'About the year 1853 it became known that Mr Colenso had been guilty of gross immoral conduct, in consequence of which he was suspended by the Bishop', etc. William could not deny this, he noted 'a Christian Bishop's sad want of charity opening up old sores', and characteristically detailed at length all the work he had done on the place. He lost the case, but got his compensation, some £300.

He woke one morning to find himself popular. The eldering man, with so many memories, who had been in the community from the first, had become something of a folk figure. A popular poem was made up about him, in the way of such communities, sung in the hotels and pubs: 'Billy C'lenso, to the tune of "Billy Barlow".' It too cited the past, but in no unkindly spirit:

> I'm sorry to say in the midst of the strife
> Some chap 'gan to meddle with his private life,
> And to skew the ex-parson proceeded to go
> Into the back numbers of Billy C'lenso.
>   Oh dear, raggedy O,
> You can't get a blush out of Billy C'lenso.

I wonder if Billy is in here tonight,
You'd know him at once by his choker so white. . .
  Oh dear, raggedy O,
  Long life to his Reverence Billy C'lenso.

Poor doggerel, it at least shows us that William never laid by
his clerical collar, or his claim to be regarded as the Revd
William.

In 1866 he ran for re-election to the General Assembly, this
time a forlorn hope against the leading figure on the Coast,
Donald McLean (who, by the way, made a large fortune, no
doubt legitimately, out of his career in New Zealand). Bishop
Williams did not fail to administer his pinprick: 'Yesterday
was the nomination day, and that fellow Colenso was holding
forth in an extraordinary way. But I am thankful to hear that
he is not likely to be returned.' Nor was he—'property, with
few exceptions, was solidly behind McLean'; and I am bound
to own, I should say a more suitable choice. Nice to note,
however, among Colenso's supporters a Cornish Trestrail.
Colenso naiveté exposed him to needless defeats at the hands
of the more sophisticated; someone said that he 'fights fair'—
too fair, I suspect.

This was the end of his political career. As a sweetener he
was awarded the job, with salary attached, of preparing a big
Maori Lexicon. This may be regarded as an expression of
favour on the part of the laity, for Williams had published a
Maori dictionary and, it appears, was the better scholar.
Colenso was not a lexicographer, let alone a philologist, nor
had he had the university training of his cousin. He was an
amateur; but what he had to offer was an intimate knowledge
of spoken Maori and its colloquial expressions, along with an
unsurpassed experience of native life, folklore and customs.
This qualified him in the view of the Assembly, and he was
voted a regular salary for the work.

Sir George Grey was himself interested in the project of the
Lexicon and encouraged it. For he too, great and good man,
was fascinated by the native culture and collected Maori
legends and folklore, on which he published a book. (We may
remark, since he was an outstanding, strong personality, that

he was almost as much a subject of controversy as the Colensos.)

Characteristically the work produced further frustrations, headaches, and some controversy. Once more Bishop Williams got in the way, this time unintentionally: in 1871 a third, improved edition of his Dictionary appeared, which took away any urgent want of a rival work. Colenso worked on in his usual fashion, compiling a heap of material. Then the Assembly did not appear keen on publication, which was delayed for some years. When they at last returned to the idea of publishing, William developed writer's cramp, and the work was never ready, left in a rough state. One fascicule only was printed, it appears. His biographers express the view that 'despite its imperfections it is unfortunate that the work was not published in the decade for which it was planned [1870s], when it would have set a standard by which the language could have been fully recorded at a period when the most learned Maori of the older generations were still alive."

In the autumn of 1877 Bishop Williams was in his last illness; Colenso went up to call on his old friend. He was not admitted. But in the February following he walked to the funeral—'such a tramp from the house to saddle, Shakespeare Road, down that road and through town, up to saddle in Milton Road and then to cemetery. I was nearly done up.' These, and other names, represented the poetic tastes of Alfred Domett who had laid out the town years before. The moment Williams was dead some inferior belittled his work. At once Colenso rushed to the defence, 'on behalf of the truth and of my dear and lamented friend.' So much had passed between them in early years and during the time of William's trouble—no doubt his last visit was in hope of a reconciliation.

In his seventies the indomitable man took on the inspectorate of schools. I expect that he was better qualified than anyone else for the job, and his suggestions strike one as sensible. He began by proposing an increase in the minimal pay teachers received. He went on to suggest that more attention be paid to teaching natural science. This was in accord with the ideas of a more famous Inspector of Schools at home, Matthew Arnold, though also it represented Colenso's own personal interest. Again, he advocated a Chair in Maori for the university—a more appropriate inflexion than some irrelevant subjects. The suggestion was not taken up.

His tours of inspection—shorter now, and by day—enabled him to take up once more his old hobby of plant collecting. We have seen that there was a vein of poetry in him. He tells us in these last years of his habit, 'in re-visiting those grand old woods, to imagine that the trees and plants, ferns, mosses and flowers recognise and smilingly welcome me. Although I lay myself open to be laughed at, wearing my heart upon my sleeve for daws to peck at, I take off my hat and salute them feelingly, and so again on leaving them for the last time.' He describes one such late scene: 'It was noon, the summer sun was high, and the view, on looking up through the interlacing foliage softly swaying in the breeze, was enchanting, every vein being translucent. And then the green of arched fronds was of such a delicate hue, such a living green without blemish. The ever-changing traceries and glints of sunlight peering down in that living bower were far beyond language.' I suppose that in every naturalist there is a poet longing to leap out.

'Thus began that long series of descriptions of specimens . . . which he usually sent to Kew—seldom duplicates for his fellow botanists in New Zealand. Questioned about this, he replied, 'I do not collect anything largely, unless it may be *hepaticae*; I keep no regular herbarium.' This of course led to his being challenged; and that of course aroused the old boy's temper: 'I, as an old and diligent fern student of fifty years, easily detect wherein you are wrong. After much consideration I have decided not to send you the Ruahine journey MSS for your new serial. We seem so diametrically opposed in our botanical views, etc, that I think I had better keep out of your arms altogether.' And so on—this to the editor of the *New Zealand Journal of Science*.

Once more, and to the last, he was involved in controversy, this time over the controversial question of species. He proposed a number of his specimens as new species, which were not recognised as such by other workers in the field. Even here there is more to be said on his side than *they* said, for it is notorious how difficult it is to define species precisely. It must have given him satisfaction to have been included with the great geologist Lyell—Bishop Colenso's stalwart friend in

England—in the dedication of Hooker's *Handbook of New Zealand Flora* in 1867.

Best of all was his election as a Fellow of the Royal Society in 1886. Here was recognition at last—for all the work he had done over half a century—and from a quarter beyond which there was no further dispute.

Chapter V

Acceptance

The last decade of Colenso's life, from his seventies to well into his eighties, was as full of activity as ever—and of the sense of life, living each moment to the full. For that we respect him – that, and the rude strength of his personality to which it was due.

It was for ever 'scribble, scribble, scribble'—mainly articles on natural science, but also pamphlets, letters—he kept up a wide correspondence—and an expansive autobiography which he did not publish. He did publish some of his reminiscences, which his biographers think well of: '*In Memoriam*: an account of visits to the Ruahine mountain range'; 'Fifty years ago in New Zealand'; 'A few historical notes concerning the early Christian church at Ahuriri'; 'Notes of early crossings of Lake Waikaremoana.' Rather touchingly his last writing, in the year of his death, 1899, was 'Memorabilia respecting some of the tin mines of Cornwall.'

Sadly enough, he does not seem to have had the opportunity to go home on a visit, as his cousin was able to do. In 1878 it was, 'this day a barque, the *Inverness*, has left us with wool for England and nearly twenty passengers. I looked at her with regret.' By this time son Willie was settled back in Penzance. In 1861 his father had at last got him back, after many efforts, just when he was standing for election to the General Assembly. His biographers suggest that it was perhaps not accidental that the Church people in the North might have thought that the return of a half-caste son might prove an embarrassment. It did nothing of the sort; 'Billy C'lenso' did not blush, but was happy to have him in time for schooling in Napier.

Writing an English-Maori lesson book for native children learning English he called it Willie's First English Book: *Ko-te A-nui a Wi hei ako maana ki te reo Ingarahi*, Wi being Willie's baby name when he first appeared to give such trouble to the father.

He was particularly fond of his love-child, always keeping him in funds. In 1878 he writes to some friends who had taken him under their wing, 'I am pleased to hear *you* are Willie's banker; be sure you don't allow him to draw all out too readily. Of course I know from him and from you all that he is saving for a yacht—all right if he can do so, and if the said yacht is a sea-worthy one, and *if he will not be too venturous.*' Certainly he himself had been venturous enough.

In 1867 his other son, Latimer, arrived on them in Napier from Auckland where he had been brought up with his mother's family. William, in his candid way, let him read the correspondence between the two parents. Now twenty-one Latimer was going to Cambridge, where he seems to have done nothing much. Oddly enough he settled too in the old Colenso home in Penzance, so strong is the pull that Cornwall exerts.

To both sons went a stream of letters, papers, scientific articles, presents, cash. 'The father did all in his power to interest his sons in his pursuits.' They seem to have had none of their own; one hears nothing of, or from, them—just ordinary humans of no interest. All that the poor old patriarch requests in return is a case of Cornish pilchards 'put up sardine-fashion.'

Once in the long intervening years he saw Ripeka again, when Willie arrived in Napier in 1861. 'That was the *first* time of my ever seeing your mother from her leaving us in '52, nearly ten years. And it was also the *last*, for I never saw her after, although for some time we continued to correspond by letter.' Her man Hamuera, whose life William had probably saved, at any rate healed him, lived on to be an old man; one does not know about Ripeka—someone remembered seeing her once on a tug-boat, 'a handsome woman with curly hair.'

And Elizabeth? She went on with the mission work, which was what she really loved, on her own. She moved to teach in a mission school in the Waikato district until 1860, when she went to England to present the chief, Pomare, to Queen Victoria. (One thinks of Cetewayo.) On her return she lived at the Bay of Islands, until in 1876 she went to the Norfolk Island Melanesian Mission, where she spent over twenty years. The pretty daughter, Fanny, married and lived an unmemorable family life—no contact with her father: she took her mother's side in the family split.

Strangest of all, in his last years Colenso came back to his clerical duties. Himself had never ceased to be Christian and to attend church—merely excluded from functioning by Bishops Selwyn and Williams. Now they were dead, and he was called on as busily as ever, in fact was needed with the increase of population, to conduct services—all the services that a deacon might take: baptising, marrying, burying, preaching. A deputation came up to Milton Road, the spacious villa surrounded by flowers on a bluff overlooking the sea, to conduct him formally to church, where he was warmly welcomed. The new bishop came down to the entrance to receive him, 'with a hearty shake hands and kind words (!!!), followed by Samuel Williams [now Archdeacon] and the Canons and the dean and the parsons', and some of the older folk. Acceptance—the old enmities laid. Home at last.

It was very right that his life should come full circle in this way, for he had come to New Zealand inspired simply by his religious belief, and for no other motive than to be a missionary. Drummed out of the Church, he had then prospered and made money; but that had not been his motive at all. Fifty years later, in the fragment of Autobiography he wrote to explain himself to son Willie, he examined his conscience.

He had seen this land, 'which was wild and savage when I came to it, made a Colony and become a rich and rising one.' He had seen 'what the many came hither for and are still coming—namely, for land, for gold [the 1860s saw a gold rush to South Island] or riches of some sort; to better their circumstances or position; for promotion, for the cause of science; for health, for ease, for the fine climate; for an idle life or to live without restraint.'

All those varied motives, Leftist historians might remember, enter into the complex process of colonisation. None of those motives had entered into Colenso's mind, any more than with his cousin, the famous Bishop of Natal. They were good men, and they went out into the world to do good.

William went on: 'I have asked myself the question, "Did any one or more of those things tempt or draw me hither?" And I can unhesitatingly and truly answer, NO. All such were never once thought of by me, had no inducements for me. I can safely say that the *only* thing which induced me to leave my country, and family and friends and come to this land—then little known and wild, without society, without civilised comforts and even common necessaries—was *to serve God* in the great mission field: *for this alone and for no other purpose.*'

When he came to the years of his troubles he came to a mystery he could not understand. 'While I cannot fathom what seems to me a great depth, or gulf, or mystery in my middle life, I can, I do look back on the past with thankfulness, and forward with increased confidence for the future.' He had the sense, as others have had, of having been directed. He felt that 'He who sees the end from the beginning—who put that right spirit into me for His work, who called me, and opened the way, and brought me forth from my native land, who always enabled me for my work of every kind, who has ever protected and delivered me from my many enemies, and led me on through good and evil, and has borne with me and all my many failings—that He will never forsake me.'

He felt that there had been a mystery in it all, the mystery of life. And he concluded from the Psalms, 'Thine eyes did see my substance', i.e. the inner man, where we have seen only the outer.

He was eighty-eight when he died on 10th February 1899. Solitary as ever, 'no wife, no child, no relative was there to mourn his passing.'

But it was found that he had remembered everybody, and how generous the man of considerable property had been all along. £2000 went to the town of Napier; he had made a much bigger offer to found a Museum, if a like sum were raised. No support was coming from the rich runholders 'with their princely domains, thousands of acres, and tens of thousands of sheep'—a last fling. So books went to Penzance, with £1000 to invest for the deserving poor. One donation to the Church had been for £400; a draft of £450 to Ridley Latimer, who rather questioned the scale of father's generosity to others. Quite considerable sums went to all those who had been named after himself—a touch of the old ego in that. For some years he had been in the habit of doling out charity to people asking for assistance, sometimes five or six a day. Like

Jonathan Swift, he lived frugally and saved on himself to give to others.

Beneath the rugged, formidable exterior there was a kind heart.

Note on Books

Bishop Colenso. Primary sources are his own works, particularly *Ten Weeks in Natal*, his *First Steps in Zulu*, and his *Pentateuch* (7 vols); *Colenso Letter from Natal*, ed. Wyn Rees. The standard biography is *The Life of John William Colenso* by Sir George W. Cox (2 vols 1888). This authoritative book has a mass of correspondence, to which all subsequent works are indebted. Excellent books are Jeff Guy's *The Heretic*, and *The Destruction of the Zulu Kingdom*; also Donald R. Morris, *The Washing of the Spears: The Rise and Fall of the Zulu Nation*. To spare the reader footnotes, most of my quotations are from these sources, unless otherwise specified; e.g. John Rogerson's standard *Old Testament Criticism in the Nineteenth Century*.

I have had the advantage of studying the volume of pamphlets on the Pentateuch controversy collected by Lord Houghton, in the library of his grand-daughter Mary, Duchess of Roxburghe, to whom I am grateful.

William Colenso. Indispensable is the biography by A.G. Bagnall and G.C. Petersen: *William Colenso: Printer, Missionary, Botanist, Explorer, Politician* (A.H. and A.W. Reed, Wellington, New Zealand, 1948), without which my account of him could not have been written. Quotations, unless otherwise noted, are drawn either from it or from the typescript of Colenso's Autobiography during the middle years which I came by many years ago—I think by Mr Petersen's kindness.

I recommend for background Keith Sinclair's admirable *History of New Zealand*, and the *Penguin Book of New Zealand Verse*, edited by my friend Allen Curnow.

Perhaps also *The Oxford History of New Zealand*, sociological in its approach; and, more lively, J.A. Froude's *Oceana*.